STORIES & REMARKS

D0878402

FRENCH MODERNIST LIBRARY

Series Editors
Mary Ann Caws
Richard Howard
Patricia Terry

STORIES & REMARKS

Raymond Queneau

with a preface by

Michel Leiris

translated and with

an introduction by

Marc Lowenthal

University of

Nebraska Press

LINCOLN & LONDON

Publication of this book was assisted by a grant from the National Endowment for the Arts.

NATIONAL
ENDOWMENT
FOR THE ARTS

Originally published as *Contes et Propos*
© Éditions Gallimard, 1981

Éditions de l'Herne has granted permission to publish "On Some Imaginary Animal Languages and on the Dog Language in *Sylvie and Bruno* in Particular," a translation of "De quelques langages animaux imaginaires et notamment du langage chien dans *Sylvie et Bruno*"

♾

Library of Congress Cataloging-in-Publication Data
Queneau, Raymond, 1903–1976.
[Contes et propos. English]
Stories and remarks / Raymond Queneau ; with a preface
by Michel Leiris ; translated and with an introduction by Marc Lowenthal.
p. cm.
Includes bibliographical references.
ISBN 0-8032-3801-0 (cl : alk. paper) — ISBN 0-8032-8852-2 (pa : alk. paper)
I. Lowenthal, Marc, 1969– II. Title.

PQ2633.U43 C5913 2000
843'.912—dc21   99-462111

A polymath pessimist, modest mathematician, and occasional bestselling author, Raymond Queneau was many things to many people. He had always remained cognizant of—if not always involved in—the significant literary movements of his time, and his influence, both as a writer and as a reader, has been enormous, if often hidden. As a writer, he touches on the full gamut of twentieth-century French literature. His early involvement with the Surrealists provided him with what he described as "the impression of having had a youth," and Isidore Isou cited Queneau's "pictogrammes" of that time period (a series of pictorial language poems) as a significant chapter in the history of Lettrism. His later relationship to postwar existentialism was assured through close friendships with Simone de Beauvoir and Jean-Paul Sartre, and if he didn't actually associate himself with the New Novelists, they did not neglect to associate themselves with his work (Alain Robbe-Grillet singled out Queneau's first novel as a precursor). But perhaps most significantly, he was a much valued member of the College of 'Pataphysics, and the College's offshoot, the Oulipo (two groups to which we shall return).

As a reader, his contributions are equally impressive.[1] Queneau was the most assiduous attendee of Alexandre Kojève's famous lectures on Hegel in the 1930s. He later assembled the notes he took into an *Introduction to the Reading of Hegel*, one of the crucial French books of philosophy of the twentieth century—a philosophy that strongly informed the work of Sartre, Jacques Lacan, and Georges Bataille, among many others. His authoritative position at Gallimard, the most prestigious publishing house in France (as reader, general secretary, and editor), guided the course of twentieth-century French letters: many young writers—Marguerite Duras, Albert Camus, and Raoul Vaneigem, to name a few—first saw print through his influence. Sideline reading hobbies included his election to the Académie Goncourt, which placed him on the panel for one of the yearly French literary awards that helped establish many an author's career.

Queneau's presence in English is by now secure: all but one of his novels have been translated, the majority by Barbara Wright and the others by no less capable and inventive individuals. His poetry has appeared less regularly; what is barely known at all, though, is his short prose: an assortment of stories, essays, or (as much of the contents of the present volume don't fall into either category) unclassifiable absurdities.[2]

As Michel Leiris mentions in his preface, we cannot really know how Queneau intended to bring the pieces of this book together. A few of his preliminary plans exist.[3] One of them hints at a possible organization of these texts into Paleolithic, Mesolithic, and Neolithic periods, but this division does not seem to bear any relation to the dates at which he wrote the texts. If a ternary structure *was* to be used, one could apply it to his career, dividing it up via the three literary or avant-garde organizations to which he had something of a card-carrying membership.

The first is Surrealism, a specter that hangs over the first two pieces of this collection. Queneau first subscribed to what was the still pre-Surrealist journal, *Littérature*, in 1921 and became affiliated with the group from 1924 to 1929, a period in which he married Janine Kahn, sister of André Breton's wife, Simone. Despite the fact that he did not figure among the expulsions of Breton's second manifesto (which condemned a number of core Surrealists to avant-garde limbo for various anti-Surrealist "crimes"), Queneau broke with his brother-in-law's autocratic rule a few months after—a rupture that Breton later claimed to have regretted.

The significance of Surrealism for Queneau rested primarily in the fact that he used it as a dialectical touchstone, negating it both as a philosophy and as the literary style into which it eventually developed. Surrealism informed the College of 'Pataphysics and the Oulipo in a similar way; the College's R. J. Mauvoisin, for example, stated for the record that the College's members were not "lyrical or surrealist exhibitionists."[4] A point that Queneau and his associates opposed in particular was the use of exclusion as a means to group solidarity. For the College and the Oulipo, inclusion was de rigueur— de rigueur mortis, even, as no distinction was made between living and dead members. As Eugène Ionesco put it: "One does not become a Pataphysician, one is a pataphysician. If you commit suicide you are a pataphysician, and if you choose not to kill yourself you are still a pataphysician."[5]

The College of 'Pataphysics has often been regarded as either an elongated hoax or an Alfred Jarry fan club. It was actually something of an alternative to the existentialism and the "engaged" literature that held sway over the French cultural scene in the 1950s. So disengaged was their attitude, in fact, that Boris Vian made it a point of pride: "Only the College of Pataphysicians does not undertake to save the world."[6] Or as Ionesco put it: "The best activity is to refrain from all activity."[7] That one could not always take such Collegiate statements at face value is evinced in the fact that several of the College's members were former Resistance fighters and that they managed to maintain ties (primarily through Asgar Jorn's dual membership) to the Situationist International, the avant-garde anarchist group arguably credited with helping instigate the events of May 1968. The College's hyperbureaucratic methods must have made a comical contrast to the Sorbonne "liberated" by the students of that turbulent summer. Yet if the College had ever taken on a political manifestation, it no doubt would have been in line with one of the many slogans that adorned the school walls of that summer: "I'm Marxist, with Groucho leanings." 'Pataphysics could have political applications, after all; in the realm of the industrial arts, for example, René Daumal early on proposed pataphysics as a "powerful deterrent, as a mode of productive activity, against attempts to rationalize labor."[8]

'Pataphysics itself was a pseudoscience created by Alfred Jarry, whose posthumous novel, *Exploits and Opinions of Dr. Faustroll, Pataphysician*, became something of a bible to the College, the way the Comte de Lautréamont's *Maldoror* had been for the Surrealists. Its most popular definition remains Jarry's own: "the science of imaginary solutions"—a science concerned not with the laws of the general, but of exceptions. Its practice was undertaken by the College's many prominent members: Jacques Prevert, Jorn, Vian, Jean Dubuffet, Max Ernst, Ionesco, and Marcel Duchamp were just some of the College's luminary "satraps." Queneau himself joined on 11 February 1950 (17 Gueules 77, according to the College's calendar), and was designated "Unique Elector" on 8 May 1959 (19 Palotin 86).

Even so, the ever-tolerant Queneau had his reservations about the College, even noting in his journal his suspicion that the College's real function was to provide a meeting place for "fairies."[9] As to their work, he once claimed that the College managed to imply more than it explained.[10] But despite these qualms, his pataphysical career fit very neatly with his way of thinking, most notably in the College's opposition to trends: as a body, they were, as His Magnificence the Vice-Curator-Founder stated, a "minority by vocation."[11] As well, the College's well-honed practice of imperturbability was second nature to Queneau, as it was to his fiction. Characters such as this volume's Gubernatis and So-and-so share a Phileas Fogg–like quality, reminiscent of Jacques Rigaut or Jacques Vaché, those most Dada of Dadaists. It is, after all, with Dada that the College had the most spiritual allegiance: the pataphysicians took the energy, chaos, and attitude of that movement and, with hermetic erudition and a calm demeanor, codified it.

At a young age, Queneau declared in his journal: "I would like to change everything while remaining the same."[12] The College went a step further; as their *Elementary Chrestomathy* states, "conscious 'Pataphysics changes nothing."[13] Or again: "questions of 'greatness' have no meaning for us, by virtue of the postulate of Equivalence."[14] But Queneau's deep-rooted interest in Eastern metaphysics, developed through a careful reading of the Chinese classics and the books of René Guenon, no doubt prepared him well for such postulates;

compare to Vian's aforementioned proclamations the doctrine of the *Tao Te Ching*: "If nothing is done, then all will be well," or "Tao abides in non-action."[15]

But what was perhaps most significant to Queneau regarding the College was not so much their philosophy as their attitude—an attitude that consciously distanced them from the Surrealists through a serious refusal to take themselves seriously. These qualities are evident in the two College-related texts of this volume: *When the Mind . . .* (a text republished by the College) and Queneau's mini-essay on the aerodynamics of addition.

It was shortly before Queneau's death in 1976 that the College underwent its self-imposed "occultation," forbidding any manifestation of pataphysical activity on the part of its members until the year 2000. This decision reinforced their secret-societal structure (it was the Surrealist's lack of occultation—their popularization—that certain College members believed had led to their decline). One of the College's many subcommittees, however, went on to achieve a public notoriety and influence that surpassed that of their umbrella organization. Queneau and François Le Lionnais cofounded the Oulipo on 22 December 1960 (22 Sable 88, the day of Caesar-Antichrist), a decision brought about in part through the difficulties Queneau was experiencing in completing his poetic flipbook-sonnet, *100,000,000,000,000 Poems*. The group (whose name stands for "Ouvoir de Littérature Potentiel," or "Workshop for Potential Literature"), brought together professional writers and mathematicians to explore, research, and create literary structures, creating a collection of individuals whom Jacques Roubaud describes as resembling a cast of characters from one of Queneau's unwritten novels. Members were known, unknown, or soon-to-be-known men and women skilled at their crafts, including Georges Perec, Harry Mathews, Italo Calvino, and Marcel Bénabou. Like the College, membership was for life and beyond. Meeting once a month for nearly forty years, the Oulipo has proven to be a sustained and fruitful collective exercise, encouraging the production of works such as Perec's *A Void* and *Life a User's Manual*, Calvino's *The Castle of Crossed Destinies*, and Mathews's *Cigarettes*. It has "anticipated" writers such as Walter Abish and Gilbert Sorrentino, and it has rediscovered literary precedents (what the Oulipo refers to as "anticipatory plagiarists") who had employed various writing constraints such as the lipogram, the cento, or homophonic translation (to name just a few of the more common exercises popularized by the group). Most importantly, the Oulipo has offered the best counterargument to the automatic-writing practices of the Surrealists, encouraging writers to, in the words of Queneau, "escape that which is called inspiration." For Queneau, the typical act of inspiration draws from limited resources. Rather than restricting the possibilities of creation, he argued, the use of artificial structure—mathematical and otherwise—opens the way to the vaster range of *potential* creation. This "potential" was not what he saw as the limited potential of the subconscious (the arena of automatic writing), but the potential of the conscious. Both approaches, of course, are capable of producing works of value. Queneau would certainly not have been prepared to dismiss Surrealist works from the literary canon: *The Magnetic Fields* or *The Immaculate Conception* are classic, influential, even beautiful works. And on the flip side, many texts produced through consciously imposed constraint could pass for Surrealist prose. One Oulipian argument would claim that the potential of the unconscious lies not so much in the possibility that it holds something unknown to the author (as Breton would have argued), but that, through its dismissal of the conscious, it may *recombine* its contents into something new, a famous example being Lautréamont's oft-cited "sewing machine-umbrella." The sewing machine and umbrella, on their own, may be everyday—their *combination* makes them surreal.

Combinatorial procedures lie at the heart of many of the Oulipo's concerns. If an argument can be construed for a Taoist reading of the College of 'Pataphysics, the Oulipo could be seen as resting upon the *I Ching*, the Chinese Book of Changes, which concerns itself with the combinations of the "10,000 things"—the sum of which, according to the Chinese classics, constituted totality. This book formed the basis of Queneau's last major work, *Morale élémentaire*, a meditative, even mystical, application of the Oulipian approach.

But even within these three groups, Queneau stood alone. What remains perhaps most distinctive about his writing is his humor, about which a word should be said. Although elected to the French Academy of Humor in 1952, and best known for his most blatantly comical works (*Zazi in the Metro* and *Exercises in Style*), Queneau never liked being labeled a humorist—an attitude much in common with that of the College. Although not averse to farce (several of their prominent members, including His Magnificence the Vice-Curator-Founder, have been elaborately nonexistent), the College sought to redefine the meaning and stature of humor and humorists in much the same way that Dada's godfather, Jacques Vaché, had decades earlier through the enigmatic spiels on "umour" that he bequeathed to his friend Breton. Erudite, vulgar and hermetic, humor was not to be taken lightly—if anything, as Prevert put it, it needed to be taken very heavily. As Daumal said in his early essay, "Pataphysics and the Revelation of Laughter": "I know and I maintain that pataphysics is not simply a joke. And if laughter often shakes the bones of us other pataphysicians, it is a terrible laughter."[16]

Harry Mathews describes the light-heartedness in Queneau's *The Skin of Dreams* as a "light-heartedness informing a radically pessimistic view of human life."[17] Pessimists, outside of Schopenhauer, are a rare breed among philosophers. Novelists and poets, on the other hand, are another matter, and Queneau crossed the lines of both camps. In his journals, Queneau described the invention of language as a means "for the sick to express their sickness"—the results being "literatorture." Such an appellation fits well with the opening of his never-written memoirs: "I am from a petit-bourgeois family: my father was anti-Semitic and my mother epileptic, my aunt practiced an underhanded euthanasia on my grandmother, one of my uncles died of delirium tremens, another managed to avoid the same by way of smoker's cancer, the third was blind in one eye."[18]

The form his humor takes, though, is rarely dark, and often opposite to its content. Queneau had no taste for "black humor," and only indulged in it for the confused parody of *We Always Treat Women Too Well*. He claimed to like all his characters, and once the wounds from his divorce from Surrealism had healed, he rarely chose assaultive purposes for his writing.

In its form, Queneau's prose resembles not so much experimental fiction as, in Constantin Toloudis's words, "fables without a moral." The fable may seem a good description, given the number of talking animals in this collection, but Toloudis is also continuing a discussion that Queneau had begun in an early essay on humor.[19] The kind of reading we adopt in a fable, Toloudis explains, involves "the expectation of a message that must be perceived as otherness, apart from the presence of the text."[20] When this "otherness" is withheld, one ends up with something like pataphysical hermeticism. But of what does this "otherness" consist? As with the occult sciences, what the fable hides, Toloudis continues, is the *truth* that it illustrates. In the realm of the tragic, Queneau points out, this "truth" takes on the form of symbolism. In the realm of humor, though, it becomes something different.

What, then, if anything, *is* being hidden within the pieces of this collection? What "otherness" lurks within these fabular Trojan Horses? Nothing much seems to happen: panic attacks arise, literally, from nothing; "In Passing" describes what *could* happen in the realm of love, but does not; the "Conversations" Queneau assembles are simply that, and his "Dream Accounts," if potentially "plentiful," are so because they are merely banal incidents transformed through a writing style. The murder in "A Bit of Glory" perhaps constitutes the biggest "event" of the collection, but it arises over the efforts of a nobody trying to get noticed. The subject of Queneau's writing often appears to be banality itself, the banality that Queneau, in speaking of Gertrude Stein, saw as being "elevated to the rank of a metaphysical value."[21] As a teenager, Queneau wrote in his journal: "I would like to find something original that is not the opposite of a banality,"[22] a paradox that well describes the odd quality of Queneau's writing.

To better understand how this banality becomes "original," one would have to look to Queneau's two philosophical predecessors: Hegel (as Alexandre Kojève understood him), and Heidegger (who had also been introduced to the French in the 1930s). Nothingness was a very original concept at the time, and Heidegger's philosophical brand of it had been cause for excitement, setting the stage for the forthcoming disaffectedness of existential bohemia. Another paradox? Nothingness might strike one as cause for boredom sooner than excitement, but as the central character of "At the Forest's Edge" states to Dino: "I'm never bored." The quadruped replies that only animals are never bored, implying that boredom is what distinguishes humans from animals. But what is boredom? Heidegger: "Profound boredom, by spreading into the depths of existence like a silent fog, strangely merges things, men and ourselves, into a general lack of differentiation."[23] If one takes Dino at his canine word, then, humans distinguish themselves from animals through their capacity to eradicate such distinctions.

This silent, undifferentiated fog runs through all of Queneau's works, whether it be within the heads of his characters or through their environments. A mist opens up "The Trojan Horse," from which the barman arises like an apparition; a fog surrounds the events of "At the Forest's Edge," which manages to swallow up both Gubernatis's companion and whatever motives may lie behind his journey (and whatever narrative intentions Queneau may have had); "Dino" starts off with a well-grounded note of ambiguity, and the dog's existence remains as defined as So-and-so's given name. It is boredom and loneliness, actually, that give rise to Dino in the first place. If forms do become defined, though, if efforts are made to rise out of banality (as in the one dramatic piece of this collection), they often only turn full circle back to their former condition: that of a formless mass, like the uncarved block of Taoism, or like the devastated ruins of "The Cafe de la France."

It is this lack of differentiation that allows Heidegger to describe boredom as the "revelation of existence in its totality."[24] One cannot be bored unless totality has been attained, unless every combination of the *I Ching*'s 10,000 things have been realized, unless every one of Queneau's *100,000,000,000,000 Poems* has been read. On a historical level, totality produces the post-Hegelian end of history, as Kojève conceived it—an end to all "events." Totality has no exterior, there is nothing exotic, destinies have all already been realized. Occupational hierarchies no longer exist: to sweep a floor is as ennobling as writing a philosophical treatise. Given such a realized "postulate of Equivalence," one is not surprised to read Queneau confess: "I've always been partial to *universality*."[25] In an early essay, Queneau stated that: "In reading many books one can accumulate riches, but to be truly rich one must renounce them, one must renounce that which Goethe called the 'infinite detail.'"[26] It is this "infinite detail" that separates totality from universality. Totality is an accumulation of all things; universality is what all things share. What, then, might induce Allen Thiher to claim that "Queneau, the novelist, has his first loyalty to the heterogeneous and the disparate"?[27] Indeed, what induces Queneau to spend several years researching the justifiably neglected writings of nineteenth-century literary heteroclites, who not only fail to figure in any canon, but have no reason to either? This is the encyclopedic Queneau, the accumulator of the 10,000 things. The most obvious argument for bringing this collection of stories out into English would be on the side of totality: the stature of Queneau is such that everything he wrote should be made available to English readers. The universalist Queneau, however, takes on an opposite view: "The partial is worth saying only to the extent that it vibrates with a germ of universality."[28] And indeed, although certain of these pieces are little more than sketches for Queneau's longer and more significant works, they all bear this same relationship to them: each one vibrates with the germ of universal humor and melancholic charm particular to Queneau.

But the tension between these two Queneaus remains. Returning to Heidegger's view of the revealed totality of boredom, one could ask what follows such boredom. This was a question over which Kojève felt some concern: what are humans to do when history has ended? Without "events," how is a man to expend his virility, how are humans to remain human and not devolve into animals? Georges Bataille's efforts to address these questions have garnered much interest in the last decade, but the issue lends itself very well to an examination in a pataphysical light. In the words of Daumal: "The individual who has known himself in his totality can momentarily believe that he is about to scatter into dust—a dust so homogenous that it will be no more than dust.... This happy earthling explodes."[29] For the pataphysician, the universal expression of totality is this explosion, otherwise known as *laughter*, and the tension posed by our two Queneaus is this same tension described by Daumal's brilliant formula:

> I am Universal, I explode;
> I am Specific, I contract;
> I *become* Universal, I *laugh*.[30]

Queneau is not jovial, his laughter is not warm, and when all is said and done, the stories and remarks of this collection are not funny—they are absurd. And as every pataphysician knows, "*evidence can only manifest itself when clothed in absurdity*."[31] It is recommended, then, that this collection be read with a very, *very* serious eye.

For their input and suggestions, I would like to express my appreciation to Jordan Stump, Eugenio Rasio, Barbara Atwood, Damon Krukowski, Alastair Brotchie, Suzanne Gauch, John Jenkins, Kelly Porter, Alan Spiegel, and Lawrence Lowenthal, as well as to the University of Nebraska Press for handling this book in such an expert manner. I would like to thank Madeleine Velguth in particular for her crucial reading of the manuscript as a whole. For further information on the composition and publication of the individual pieces in this collection, I refer the reader to the notes.

Marc Lowenthal

Published some five years after Raymond Queneau's death, *Stories and Remarks* represents the fulfillment of an express intention of the author, who wished to assemble under this title a certain number of prose writings that, taking only their dimensions into account—the most modest, even when they're not what he called "texticles"—one can consider as minor.

These texts, all marked with a touch of cold absurdity that tends to side them with what André Breton called "black humor,"[1] but whose wild diversity attests above all to an encyclopedic mind open to singularity—unpublished texts as to the oldest one, scattered as to the others—have been arranged chronologically (for lack of a preestablished framework or any other information that might have provided the basis for a more significant organization) by the painter Jean-Marie, son of the writer, and Robert Gallimard, who took charge of publishing this collection. Now, among these texts, classified without any preconceived idea and focusing on the simplest of them, it so happens that the first and the last (it seems to me) cast a curiously precise light on what anyone, his attentive reader at the very least or whoever like myself had the chance to maintain a long and friendly relationship with him, can regard—without claiming to have considered from every angle this personality, made all the more captivating by the intricacy of his facets—as the *manner* of Raymond Queneau, his manner of being and, consequently, his manner of writing.

And reaching Manila, first sign of the Orient, Stobel understood how wandering had only served to bring him back to places he already knew. It is in a story entitled *Destiny,* written in 1922 and thus previous to everything by Raymond Queneau that has been published up to today, that these lines appear—prophetically one could say—these lines that, from the outset, illustrate a very consistent trait of his: a distrust of exoticism, a distrust evident in the whole of what he wrote, which is usually situated, when there is localization, in an urban or suburban milieu as typically French as could be made, as much by the author's nationality as by his language—in which his Sunday-best writing as well as his everyday voice is crafted—and, for this same individual whose patronymic links him prosaically to the dog and the oak, a general way of thinking that couldn't help but contribute to his freeing himself rather quickly from Surrealism, a movement that an intelligence as keen as his own was able to regard as a kind of escape toward exotic mental regions, apparently foreign to those where common sense prevails, insofar as they are for this reason a source of delectable strokes of inspiration, but such that what is revealed there is only what one brought oneself. If to embark in one way or another for *yonder* is in the end only to go to the same thing, is it not *here* that one must endeavor to find this elsewhere—or this piquancy—failing which, our existence is lacking in all flavor? In other words, if all wandering brings one back to places one already knows, why not take the places one knows as pretexts for wandering?

With Raymond Queneau, who seems to have been driven to become a pataphysician and then an oulipian through a certain taste for ironic speculation and experimentation, things never take place in the distances our naïveté values so much. Of course, in his life as in his inventions, he did not always stay confined to places familiar to him, but if he happens, for instance, to take his readers to Ireland, it is under the comical pseudonym of Sally Mara, to an Ireland of pure convention and parody, and if among several trips he took one to Greece (of which the title of one of his last books reminds us), it was not at all with the intention of wandering but rather, judging by the content of this book, as if such a return to sources had led him to put some ideas in order rather than to marvel at what was only a superficial change of scenery. In the first case, the exoticism only had derisory value, and in the second, there wasn't even any since, for any European endowed with a bit of culture, to go to Greece is in a sense to return to the house in which one was born.

Whereas others ventured into a hazardous explosion of our depths (which for a large part was the Surrealist project), Raymond Queneau did not go miles from anywhere to do what he was able to do at home, and he made cock and bull stories arise from banality itself. Thus, in his *Stories and Remarks*, he shows us, among other peculiar elements of a world that one could swear was everyday, a dog who starts up a conversation with a customer in the very ordinary dining room of a provincial cafe, as well as a horse, Trojan no less, having a drink in a high-class bar. Texts that, in their realist content, present a literature of the fantastic that is in a way natural rather than a literature of the supernatural that makes a deliberate break with positivity, whereas others—in a similar vein—have more, if one can say such a thing, of an intellectual fantastic element (quietly preposterous considerations). Writings duly *written* in which the person responsible never chases after this utopia: to take literature beyond the limits that its nature lays down from its origins.

If Raymond Queneau the poet is sometimes not averse to taking a breathtaking flight (see in particular the impressive *Explanation of Metaphors*, which actually "explains" nothing, other than the power of discourse when it is taken to its extreme), Raymond Queneau the writer of prose generally operates in a down-to-earth manner, being less an admirer of the *elsewhere* than an imaginative stroller through the turns and detours of a most prosaic reality that he shifts about and disorientates, without this modification—he's an artist, but not at all idealizing—making it lose any of its immediacy. Rather than travel in pursuit of exoticism, without even knowing where you are going, is it not better to change (distance, exoticize) what is close to you and what you know only too well? In short, to invert the movement, in the sense of a counterexoticism: not to leave familiar shores for foreign lands, but to see to it that the familiar suddenly becomes foreign. It is an operation in which language is the instrument and that concerns ideas just as well as things, since in his poems as well as in his novels, one sees Raymond Queneau sometimes take, as a point of departure, a reality belonging to this world (which will remain the everyday world whatever torsion it undergoes), sometimes a commonplace of universal literature and of all time (embellishing on it as in music one embellishes on variations on a theme). Not to disorder, it will seem to the reader, but to disorbit the writing by drawing it (which is only, when all is said and done, to bring it back to the fold) toward spoken language and by sometimes striking a fatal blow at orthography, which then becomes more or less phonetic as if to place into the sentence—collage-style—a little block of sonorous reality and, at the same time, to disfigure (that is, make unrecognizable at first sight), indeed, in the strict sense, to *uproot* the expression thus tampered with. It also happens—*Stories and Remarks* offers examples—that the writing utterly liberates itself and works for itself, not by transcribing realities (whether true or imaginary), but by creating, by way of puns or other language games, realities with no other substance than the grammatical proposition that asserts them. With Raymond Queneau, however resistant he may be to the carelessness of automatism, it is ultimately writing as such that has the force of law.

Instead of relying on a sacrosanct inspiration supposedly coming from the depths, he absorbs what he sees when looking lucidly around himself and, seeking the picturesque in inanity itself, deals with things retained while casting his speech in the mold of this rhetoric to the powers of which the note accompanying the final sequence of *Stories and Remarks* implicitly pays homage, dated 1973 and intended to show that the "dream account" practiced so prolifically by the Surrealists was in fact nothing but a new literary genre: *Of course none of these dreams are any more real than they are invented. They are simply minor incidents taken from wakened life. A minimal effort of rhetoric seemed sufficient to give them a dreamlike aspect.*

An open use of rhetoric (here to transform into dreams what had not been) and compositional devices given to the unusual, such is one of the aspects of demystification that Raymond Queneau—a great classical author, which doesn't keep him from being antiestablishment—will have undertaken; sharp as his sense of the burlesque may have been, it was most certainly not a question of ridiculing literature but, with complete artisanal honesty, of putting it back in its proper place—one of the sturdiest places, incidentally, when one no longer has any romantic illusions about it.

Michel Leiris

1. Translation

Ancient values! Ancient truths! Such are the clichés hatched in studious evenings. He's a young man—in bygone days, they say, hard-working and learned and wealthy. His name, no one knows why, is Christian Stobel. His childhood and first flush of youth are even less known to us than his fetal life. But a day comes when conversion fulfills him. A new integration reveals some new function. A fortuitous encounter, an act of chance have changed habits that had seemed forever confirmed; and a journey confirms his anxiety.

2. Port

Having no taste at the moment for any sort of study, Christian Stobel went to Le Havre. He lives in a hotel on the rue Racine, where women's corpses are sometimes found, and where men arrange to meet. He writes antiopes. The overwhelming smell of the tarred sails delights him as much as the rectilinear length of the lines. He seeks an adventure; he doesn't find one—due to his inexperience; and then, he doesn't have a lot of imagination either.

3. Bohemians

One day as he's wandering in the countryside surrounding this city, tired from a long walk, he sits down and gazes at the small valley and hill facing him. In the distance, gypsies appear on the luminous road coming out of the depths of the woods. Four caravans move toward the coolness of the valley. Men are walking alongside, but they are still only black shapes, like block capitals. Imbued with the light of the sun, they vanish into a new darkness, crossing the market town curled up at the bottom of the valley and along the road, like an old white cat, then appear, again, more defined, at the near bend in the road. The troupe passes, imbuing the ground with the sweat of their feet—the men, bronzed and brawny, the women, tattered and torn, children, carriages, horses.

"We come from all lands and we're going to Saintes-Maries de la Mer where we meet every year. Nomads of the enigma, we trail our mystery across the unastonished countrysides and the fluid towns. Transfigured by our ambulations, we live with contempt for the immobile and the memory of gigantic, metallic green snakes."

At the bend in the road, they disappear. Stobel gets up and leaves. He returns to Paris. Some discussions with an enigmatic metaphysician suggest uncountable possibilities to him. Following which, he abandons studies, family, friends, Paris, then France.

Comrades! My dear friends, don't you find that this Stobel is quite the diaphanous, quite the translucid character? He passes by and already no one can remember anything more of him; and as for me, I'd prefer anything else to these naive stories I'm relating to you.

4. Memory

On the ship, Stobel was shelling some orange pips. He was thinking: "Nights of isles. Nights of coasts. Nights of cliffs. If only I had loved the dormer windows of old tumbledown cottages, the lust of exotic dances and the geometry of machines! All our love affairs of eighteen are over. I hauled my bewildered silences along the roads strewn with ancient prejudices. The cracks in the wall no longer let their tones pass through. The cross has darkened on the detour routes. The everlasting flowers leave for other tombs."

5. Music

Just like the undefined swarming of the numberless multitudes of the Orient, like the great mass of inexhaustible peoples, like the infinitude of crowds, sources of races, fountains of invasions—diverse patterns superimpose themselves on the principal rhythm, some expressing killings and complicated lusts, others the calm of the Sages and the cosmic charity of the Ascetics.

Paintings—in which rain and the perspectives of mountains symbolize the Infinite—argued with their calligraphed design. The music was still continuing its multiple rhythms, in which all individuality seemed to lose itself. How can one remain *someone* before the antiquity of these Ancestors, the infinitude of their wisdom, the multitude of individuals. One must lose oneself! One must be one with Tradition, Race, the ancient Earth, and the ineluctable Principles.

6. Cinema

On the shores abandoned by insalubrious crabs, the thought of ill-fated destinies bustles about the mossy rocks, which the waves have modeled into hilarious and phallic shapes, no doubt intended to make the bathing girls muse in their swimsuits: blue, red, green, yellow, black, or white, all in accordance with the destinies guiding their lives—or the color of their lovers' ties.

If Stobel wanders along the beach, amid the eccentric or photogenic bathing girls in their swimsuits, it is not that the desire for women torments him, nor that the climate enchants him. He is only there to fulfill the destiny that he set for himself, and, before leaving, he contemplates the mossy rocks with their phallic shapes, the thighs and buttocks of the bathing girls, the sand, gray, white, or bronze depending on which direction the sun is leaning, and the sea where the mermaids, dead for so long, seem to awaken to the wind of destinies suitable for the Pacific Ocean.[1]

7. Navigation

Three continents have wearied him—and now he is on the lookout for a yacht to the South Sea Islands. He never managed to flee from himself. The earth isn't that big—whatever they may say. And reaching Manila, first sign of the Orient, Stobel understood how wandering had only served to bring him back to places he already knew. Even if he had run off to the forests of South America or the ' steppes of Siberia, he would always end up finding something he had already fled.

He was thinking in this manner, seated on a deckchair upon his yacht. He gazed at this tropical land and this sea that reminded him that he had already passed through not far from there, when he had traveled from Singapore to Hong Kong.

His mind is surrounded. One can only follow curved lines on the earth's sphere that, when extended, always meet. At this point on the earth, he comes up against the already seen. He doesn't want to return to former experiences. He cannot bow again before the ever-lasting and disconcerting civilizations of the Orient.

He believes he has gone round the world, explored all civilizations, all thoughts (just about). He doesn't want to return, he doesn't want to stay.

"My will and my wealth gave me things, I guided my destiny and now my will comes up against itself. May things be hereforth the masters of myself! May I depend on possible circumstances!"

At Palembang, there's a bar for sale. Stobel buys it. He disperses the remains of his fortune and makes a gift of his yacht to the captain, who has since been selling holothurians to the mandarin epicures of Shanghai.

One can imagine him becoming an opium smoker, alcoholic or ataxic, or having a wife and kids who will go to school in Melbourne, or else converting to the Catholic religion. All that is of no importance.

Anyway, this story is quite tedious. It's a good thing it's finished. Whether you like it or not, I couldn't care less.

NOTICE

This first volume of the Collection Q,[1] which very explicitly aims at science's RECREATION, brings a generative text back to light.

Published in 1929 (merdre 56 in reality) in a journal that one can qualify as Belgian—at the same time as *The Treasure of the Jesuits*, Messrs. Aragon and Breton's treatise on dramatic art—this inestimable compendium opened such infinite perspectives that no one even perceived them. It is only today, after the full development of the theories of Canon Lemaître (who at that time was still a simple priest, but was already very congenitally and mathematically Belgian, like Bosse-de-Nage, our Starosta),[2] and even more, if such a thing is possible, after the strange upheaval brought on by the theories of the *Galactic and Supergalactic Turbulence*, which have given us, and Monsieuye Sainmont[3] in particular, much to ponder over this year, it is only, I say, enlightened by an Astronomy that has passed from the logico-mechanical stage to the mathematico-aberrant stage since the opening of the gates of the infinite by Hubble in 52-1925—it is only after all these detours that we can now gauge the depth and feel the translucent viscosity of the prophetic intuitions that ferment in these pages, and that in some fashion are the image of the Cosmic Viscosity itself as assumed by the most daring researchers of our time. Pataphysics precedes always, and by far.

Oktav Votka[4]

Removable Moderator

(provisional)

of the Corps de Satraps

I

When the mind, abandoning research with an immediate practical aim, devotes itself to the study of the

PHYSICAL WORLD

its diversity disconcerts it to such a degree that only the principles of relativity or of enumeration offer themselves as explanations for the said diversity, the preceding possessive of which applies to the researching mind as well as to the researched physicality. The classification into living and nonliving things is at the basis of physics as well as chemistry, for the laws of falling bodies, which model themselves on feathers or lead, never take as an example the guinea pig or the snail. Why are experiments on the laws of gravity never made with living beings, a pigeon, for instance, or an eagle? There is a lack of honesty here in the physicist.[5] Moreover, since a majority of objects do not fall

> (dust suspended in the atmosphere,
> birds,
> clouds,
> balloons,
> airplanes,
> planets,
> stars,
> archaeopteryxes (*in their time*),
> etc. . .)

there is therefore no reason for others to fall. In actual fact, a thing makes its way toward the center (?) of the earth (??) only if it meets a

BVFFER

A buffer is an invisible, imaginary, and fallacious being that lies in wait for objects deprived of physical support and clings to them. Then it flies down to the earth and lays them there; then it goes off again. Thus the illusion of a fall is created, but no such thing has occurred: it is only a sort of transport, I would even say a method of locomotion.

In a higher course of lectures, we shall study buffers specialized in the fall of leaves and those that take the form of age and death.

II

THE WORLD

is a tablet dropped in a glass of water.

AIR AND WATER

are identical in relation to earth; ether and water, in relation to the world: mountains result from the disaggregation of earth under the action of air.

PLANETS

result from the disaggregation of the sun under the action of water (*ether*).

SATELLITES

are air bubbles contained in the tablet, which escape when it disaggregates, carrying along certain solid particles. Aerolites and comets seem to be exclusively solid and of an explosive nature.

Thus

THE MOON

is hollow.

There is a tablet at the bottom of the world that, when disaggregating, projects stars into the sky.

ALEXANDRINE

The star is lost below and the skies are water.

THE EARTH

is also below; it is—if you like—what made the stars.

PARTICLES

that burst forth fall back again and return to their former domicile. Islands and continents originate in this manner.

> The earth is a sunken ship,
>
> the moon is a drowned man,
>
> comets are wreckage.

THE TABLET

is a volcano, its own disaggregation the lava, particles A the smoke, particles B the pumice.

It is also the dead man who falls into the municipal earth of the cemeteries, particles A being the cries of despair of the buried one who is breathing, particles B being the most quickly sated worms that gallop to the surface in order to take the air at the feet of the nearby cypress trees. The male twirls his cane and the female embroiders cushions in the shape of a fan.

ASTRONOMY

is a miscarried science, and the sun continues to revolve around the earth. Preoccupations about those light-years never interested anyone but popularizers, and the seemingly incalculable number of stars has nothing to do with the infinite.

Astronomy, vacillating and weak, takes refuge in institutions of an obscene shape, known as observatories: a cupola split in two, into which a telescope inserts itself.

THE IDEA OF THE MOON

is a concept in the form of a pear.

Likewise,

the CONCEPT of the SVN

has the form of an egg.[6]

Louis-Philippe is the moon-king.
Louis XIV, the egg-king.

In the form of a PEAR:
 royalty,
 the League of Nations,
 the bourgeoisie,
 the Civil Code,
 the integrity of the land,
 the flag.
In the form of an EGG:
 the pope,
 Christ,
 the Unknown Soldier,

baptism,
circumcision,
the Vatican.

War is a concept in the form of a cigar clipper;

the morning twilight in the form of a death's head (the alarm clock, for instance, is supported by two tibias);

the umbrella in the form of a typewriter.

There are also ideas in the form of sardine cans: rebuses, houses, dead languages, modern languages.

VSELESS
to continue
it is enough that I have opened the way to
future and toothsome research workers
(the concept of research
being in the form of a
TOOTH).

It was quite difficult for M. G. to obtain an entry card to the Bibliothèque Nationale: no degree backed up his application, no research legitimized his request, and yet this was really the only place he could achieve his ends. Any other way of proceeding would have been futile and inefficient, doomed to too many hazards. M. G. thus passed a whole summer without managing to support his application, when one autumn day, passing before some official billposting, he noticed an ad for the École du Louvre. He understood, enrolled (although until then he had never been interested in this manner of study), studied the art of the Middle Ages and epigraphy, and finally, a holder of a diploma, he was able to obtain a library card, the one that gave him access to the Work Room.

The first day that he went there, he sat down somewhat at random; it was before the war, in the days when one could still choose one's seat. Then he looked around, got his bearings, learned the operation of this big machine. There were notably the catalogues, which he had to know how to use, numerous catalogues, some printed, others handwritten, still others photographic, some on cards, others not, in alphabetical order or in order of subject: in short, an entire apprenticeship to serve. Once he had understood a bit of it, M. G.'s first concern was to find his name in the general catalogue; he found it; for him, this was a very great emotion, a very intense joy. With his hand holding volume 48 open at the page, raising his eyes to the ceiling, he dreamed for a few moments, and he smiled. There were the three works he had published, well described, with their numbers: the *Renewal of the Earth through the Exclusion of Newton*, Lyon:

Lenglumé, 1841, in-8° of VIII–246 pp., R. 24111, the *Limit of the Heavens Reduced to its Apt Expression*, Lyon: Lenglumé, 1843, in-8° of IX–351 pp., R. 24112 and the *Newtonian Night until Now Widespread on the Earth and Henceforth Obliterated by the Great Day of Truth*, Caen: Ledoyen, 1859, in-8° of XL–674 pp., R. 26700.

M. G. didn't tire of reading and rereading these few bibliographic lines—all that remained of him on this earth in the way of glory, for in all the dictionaries and catalogues that he had been able to consult, he had not found any trace of his name or of his work, nor for that matter in any treatise, any history book.

The second part of his program was carried out in the following manner: he filled out the three necessary cards and asked for his three books. About an hour later, an employee designated to this task brought them to him. They were black with dust; M. G. shook them off, then saw that they had not even been consulted, ever; their pages were not even cut. M. G. hung his head heavily while absentmindedly thumbing through his works; so, he had never been read—at least not here. But what good was hoping that he had been read elsewhere. No one had ever looked into his wild imaginings—and yet he recalled the moments of genius that enlightened his sojourns in Lyon, then in Caen, the fervor with which he wrote, the enthusiasm that consumed him. Then, after the publication, the complete failure, the silence. Then M. G. had died, hoping for at least something from posterity. He now saw that posterity had never concerned itself with him.

He left the Nationale that day, weighed down by disappointment and despair. He wandered all night, thinking over what he had to do. The darkness of Paris saw him in different quarters murmuring over the examination of his problem. In the morning, at opening time, he was there, he went in, he began to observe. His observations were practiced methodically for several days, several weeks, several months. He showed such discretion that no one noticed his surveillance. What was this old bearded gentleman interested in? The death of Louis XVI. And this young blond girl? Jansenism.

And this other one? This other one? This other one? Not a single scholar, not one, seemed to have conceived of a project that M. G.-ian literature could touch on or relate to. Months passed. M. G., with a shrewd eye, continued to watch the intellectual life of the work room.

One reader, however, ended up intriguing him, for he couldn't make out any link between the different authors for whose numbers he saw him hunting. Yet he couldn't take him for someone who would have picked and chosen at random in the catalogue's riches, for he did seem to be pursuing a well-defined line of research. After a certain time, M. G. was able to ascertain that these authors were all French, of the nineteenth century and, as far as he could judge, completely unknown. He hesitated some more, continued to observe, and nevertheless had to conclude that he, himself, was in the position of interesting the unknown reader, being French, ondivigesimal, and what was more (alas!), unknown. As for the subject matter of his works, it was as presentable as those of the others: no science seemed not to interest the character.

He now had to meet him; and for that, he had to use cunning.

He followed the character, observed his behavior, took note of his customs, calculated his habits, inferred his tastes; he kept a close watch on him. The character had no friends and hardly any acquaintances; he got close to one of these, who, one day, introduced them to each other. They chatted. M. G., confident in his inquiry, guided the conversation, and soon the character confessed the nature of his work, a quarto probably of some six hundred pages, bibliography and all, which would deal, uncondensed, with obscure Frenchmen of the nineteenth century, a vast subject. M. G., filled with emotion, then said to him:

"Do you know M. G.?"

The scholar didn't know him.

"He wrote this, this, and this work," said M. G., citing the titles.

"No, I don't know him," said the scholar, "I don't know him. Very interesting," he murmured.

And he pulled a notebook from his pocket to take notes. He wrote down titles and name.

Over all the days that followed, M. G. was happy. But the next time they met, the scholar said to him:

"What was your guy's name again? Would you believe it, I lost the card."

M. G., bitter, again gave him the information.

The next time they met, the scholar said to him:

"Very interesting, your guy's very interesting. I'm going to devote about four or five pages of my book to him."

And M. G. was happy again. So, he wouldn't completely die! His name would remain among men, not only in the simple and pure appearance of an inscription in the Bibliothèque Nationale's catalogue, but also in the distinguished form of a note devoted to him by a scholar of merit in some masterly quarto. He was happy. He would live forever, or at least for a very long time—a very, very long time. He didn't want to think so far ahead. All the same, he could continue his posthumous life in this way for hundreds of years, perhaps thousands. Did the pure chance of the catalogues not allow one to still cite Greek writers of whom not even a line remained? So why not him? Let us suppose that all this civilization disappears, and that nothing more remained of it, pure destiny, than a torn fragment of the scholar's compilation, and that this fragment was precisely the one that concerned him. Then he would survive, alone. Why not? He was happy.

The following times that he met the scholar, he asked him for news of his book. The book was moving along, soon it was almost finished, then there was nothing more than a few adjustments to make. It was going to the printer's when its author lost the manuscript. Fed up, he abandoned his research and retired to some land that he had in the vicinity of Paris.

M. G. paid him several visits, to encourage him. He was still hoping that the other was going to start over. But no, the other didn't want to, didn't want to hear about it. M. G., seeing all possibility of surviving in the spirit of men vanish, felt himself weaken little by little and disintegrate. In the supreme rage of his near and total death, he concentrated all the strength remaining to him to suffocate the scholar. Who died. As for himself, he went on scattering himself bit by bit, he drifted away, nothing of him remained, ghosts have no ghosts. (Is that so certain?)

" 'Taint funny pulling a trick like that on Palm Sunday!" grumbled a slattern of the female sex, picking up a dog turd deposited in front of the office door; said female slattern then went to find a cloth and some water to wash away the very last traces of the canine misdeed. During her absence, a man of some forty years had entered.

"I would like to see a room," he said, politely greeting the servile being, who went unhurriedly in quest of the manageress.

This stout person, sniffing out her prey, smiled:

"You would like a room, monsieur?"

"Yes, madame."

"For one or two people?"

"For one. It's for me."

"This would be for a long time?"

"For at least three months."

Now isn't that interesting.

"I have number 6 vacant on the first floor and number 30 on the second."

"I would like a very quiet room."

"Oh, monsieur, it's very quiet here! The neighborhood is very quiet and my boarders are also very quiet; a family from Brest, very good people, a nun . . ."

"You really guarantee the quietness of your hotel?"

"But of course, monsieur."

She laughed to show how clearly evident it was, as if evidence made one laugh.

"You want to see number 6 and number 30?"

She guided him through the maze of corridors. It was an ancient boardinghouse, established in the time of the Holy Alliance.

Through the windows of number 30 (there were two), one could see a courtyard strewn with some chestnut trees that the spring, said to be late that year, had not yet caused to bud. The visitor sniffed at the slightly mildewed atmosphere, felt the pillows (they're feather, he remarked in a low voice), glanced vaguely at the bathroom, and pinched his lower lip between the thumb and the index finger of his right hand. He made no other remark and asked to see number 6.

Number 6 was still occupied, but would be vacant in the evening. The current occupant seemed to be a rather heavy consumer of Vittel water. This room had a curious feature: the bathroom window opened out onto the street.

"If the noise of the cars bothers you, you can close the bathroom door," said the manageress. "It's very practical."

The visitor was looking about him without saying anything. He coughed, opened the window, shut it again. Then he felt the pillows.

"They're feather," he said.

The manageress did not reply, seeing nothing that could be subject to dispute.

"Couldn't they be removed?"

"Removed?"

"Yes, feathers bother me. Couldn't these pillows be removed?"

The manageress did not understand in the slightest, but she knew her job.

"Of course, monsieur. Of course, they'll be removed."

He looked about him. He examined the bathroom carefully. He came back into the room. He made up his mind.

"I'll take this one."

"Oh, it's very nice. It's very quiet, it looks onto the courtyard. If the noise of the street bothers you, you only have to close the bathroom door. It's very practical."

"Yes, it's very nice."

"And you'll be staying three months?"

"At least. I hope you'll let me have it at a reduced price."

They went back down to the office haggling over this issue. They finished by coming to an agreement. The manageress proffered her weight upon a chair that groaned.

"I'm going to ask you to fill out a guest history card, monsieur."

He did so speedily, without hesitation, like a man used to doing so. Then he refused to pay right away, preferring to wait until the following day. He left, bowing low.

The history card offered nothing of interest. The manageress put it with the others; she finished her afternoon by listening to Radio Toulouse.

Around seven, the guest reappeared. He was smiling in a self-conscious manner.

"I changed my mind. If it doesn't trouble you, madame, I would prefer the other room, the one that looks fully onto the courtyard."

"You're right, monsieur; it's certainly quieter than the other."

"But I wouldn't want to cause you any trouble."

"It's no trouble at all, monsieur. The colonel's brother was to sleep there tonight, but I'll give him number 6. It's all the same to him, for one night."

"And what's this room's number, the one that overlooks the courtyard?"

"Number 30."

"Number 30. Very good."

"When you come in, the light's under the mirror, on the right."

He bowed and left.

"Eh, say, go get the case in number 6 and carry it to 30."

The slattern, struggling, lugged the case through the corridors.

"I tell you," she said, "this monsieur's got stones in this here case."

Then she went to wolf down the swill that made up her meal.

Around eleven, number 30 returned. He took his key from the rack and went up. The manageress watched him, but discovered nothing peculiar. She got back into her solitary bed, for she was a widow; the slattern climbed up to her garret. Little by little, the whole hotel went to sleep, the colonel's brother, the nun, the family from Brest.

The manageress got up at 6:30; at 7:00, she was seated at her desk and was starting to read the paper. This lapse of time sufficed for her grooming activities, her clothing efforts and the manducation of her breakfast. Nose bearing an unsteady pince-nez, she was thus in the midst of savoring the account of the murder of the concierge of the Plaisance public baths, when a knock-knock, discrete but very decisive, made her stop her reading. It was number 30.

"Good morning, monsieur," she said with a nicely manufactured smile.

"I'm sorry, madame," said the other, "I'm leaving."

The managerial rictus collapsed.

"You're leaving?"

"Yes, I can't stay."

"It wasn't quiet?"

"Oh yes, madame, it was very quiet, very quiet."

"Then what's the matter? Something's the matter. If something's the matter, you have to tell me."

"Nothing's the matter."

Her countenance was distorted for a moment, then regained an acceptable appearance.

"It's the pillows, then!" exclaimed the manageress. "They weren't removed. That's it: the pillows weren't removed!"

"No, madame, they were removed."

"Then I don't understand. I don't understand. You told me you'd be staying three months. And this room's very quiet, isn't it?"

"Yes. Yes. It's quiet. But I had an impression. You understand, when you have an impression . . ."

He made a gesture that seemed devoid of meaning to the manageress. The latter, uncomfortable, smiled stupidly.

"How much do I owe you?" he asked.

"For one night, thirty francs."

He took out a hundred franc bill and collected the change without saying anything. The manageress was looking at him. He again made a gesture.

"You understand, I can't stay. I'm very sorry."

"I'm the one that's sorry. Goodbye, monsieur."

"Well, there you are . . ."

He abruptly seized his case, raised his hat and left. Outside, he hesitated a moment. Not a single taxi was passing by. He crossed and vanished a little further on, at the corner of the avenue.

The slattern, who was polishing a piece of furniture, exclaimed:

"What do you make of that guy!"

"I sure get some characters," said the manageress.

"He's nuts."

"He must be a neurotic. I'm glad he left."

"He had stones in his case," sniggered the slave. "Stones!"

Having thus formulated the result of her cogitations, she went back to rubbing, with increased fervor, the piece of furniture designated for her incomprehensible zeal by the very wise orders of the manageress.

I

24 June

A young Frenchman by the name of So-and-so, finding himself hard up, was glumly walking down Boulevard Edgard Quinet, along the Montparnasse cemetery, when he was accosted by a rather seedy-looking old man, almost a beggar.

"Things aren't going well, eh? They're not going well, eh?" said this old-timer.

"Can't say they are," replied So-and-so.

"I'll wager that money's your problem."

"You said it."

"What would you be prepared to do for money?"

"Anything."

"Even a burglary?"

"Why not?"

"Follow me."

They went down the Boulevard Raspail toward the Lion of Belfort.

"An old pensioner lives on the sixth floor," explained the beggar. "He keeps all his money at home. Every evening he goes out to play a game of manille. The concierge is always away from 8:00 to 8:30. In other words, the job's a cinch. This is it," he added, stopping before a lovely modern apartment building and with a nod of his head pointed out the pensioner's apartment.

"Don't make faces like that. You're going to draw attention."

The old-timer shrugged his shoulders.

"If you say so."

He went up to the door and rang the bell.

"What are you doing," So-and-so asked, alarmed.

"I live here," replied the old-timer with a smile.

The door opened; he reshut it behind him, carefully. So-and-so wandered off, calculating the square root of 123,456,789. To pass the time.

II

3 July

Returning from the races, the two Smith brothers had taken a taxi with a young Frenchman by the name of So-and-so. They had come out ahead; he had probably lost. They got out at the Opera with the intention of going for a drink at the Pam-Pam. The taxi, paid, disappeared in the direction of the Palais-Royal. It was then that the elder of the Smith brothers, his name was Arthur, noticed that he no longer had his billfold. His younger brother, whose name was also Arthur, suggested that he had probably left it in the taxi. An inspector from the Criminal Investigation Department who by chance happened to be there took an interest in this whole affair, informed them of his occupation, and bragged of recovering, in very little time, the lost billfold.

"Recovering a billfold lost in a taxi, that's child's play," he asserted.

"Excuse me," said So-and-so. "Before starting your investigations, I would like to be searched. I want no suspicion weighing upon me."

"But no one suspects you," said the Smith brothers in a heartfelt chorus.

"I want to be searched," maintained So-and-so in a bombastic tone.

"It's only to please you," said the inspector, who found in the young man's pockets not only the elder Smith's billfold, but that of the younger Smith as well.

Everyone was dumbfounded. So-and-so bolted.

"There's no use running," the policeman cried out. "I know who you are. I'll catch you when I want."

From the other side of the boulevard, So-and-so yelled out:

"No, you won't catch me!"

At that moment a Hispano 54 CV was passing by; it had just won

First Grand Prize of Honor at the competition for Automobile Elegance. So-and-so leapt in and smiled.

"Ah, to die in a Hispano," he murmured blissfully and, taking a revolver from his pocket, killed himself.

What a dirty snob!

I have no distinct memory of the dog's color; not even of his breed. I never specified whether he was a red basset hound or a black Brie shepherd, a white poodle or a wolfhound. His name was simply Dino. On the road he went looking for the stones I would throw for him and brought them back to my feet. That took place along the roads of Portugal; there were generally two or three windmills along the horizon; sometimes Dino would shake himself in the dining room, near the vineyard; or else we would walk along the cliffs, clinging to a little footpath on which we never encountered anyone but customs officers, the Atlantic waves crashing below, with no boats or bathers due to the currents. During meals Dino would sit up and beg for a lump of sugar or a piece of meat. The other hotel guests would look at us or, rather, look at me, since Dino didn't exist; but they would only demonstrate a polite attention, betraying a civilized skepticism that preferred to doubt the value of perception rather than be forced to tackle the difficult issue of the mind's singularity.

Even in the days when I mingled with a class of people who were not in the least ordinary and displayed themselves as such in various ways, I never had a taste for eccentricity, and now, some ten years later, I still wonder why I had adopted this silent and docile animal, who, to all the traits of the canine species, added the remarkable talent for invisibility. I remember clearly that I did not yet possess him on leaving Havre, and I am sure that he had not yet started to dog my footsteps on the ship. He was not in Vigo, when we nearly scraped our stern on the stone blocks of the pier; nor do I see him in Porto. Nor do I see myself in Porto, for that matter, save on my return, two months later. In Lisbon the hotel at which I stayed would certainly not have accepted such a dog. And anyway, why was I going to Lisbon? By resolving the issue of my displacement, shall I perhaps make headway into the cause of the doggy? I had no special reason for going to Portugal. One, a remote one, arose from a documentary viewed at *Parisiana* a few years beforehand, which showed the beauties of Portuguese baroque. Others might not have existed. Moreover, I always thought it was from a love of architecture that I went to Portugal; and then, I had to go somewhere.

No need for a dog in Lisbon. The automobiles, beautiful and swift, would have quickly run him over! All kinds of sights led me away from the usage of a quadruped companion. The hot, noisy nights would have been heavy and thankless for the poor animal; he would never have dared do his business upon the magnificent tiles of the public squares. Dino only appeared, this is certain, when, weary of the pleasures of the capital, I came to rent a room in a little village near the sea. It was a boardinghouse type of hotel. There was a Portuguese naval officer, the proprietor's daughter (Portuguese), and other people (also Portuguese), of whom I have not the slightest bit of memory; and then, there was Dino.

When I think about it, this animal could not have been very big; it seems to me that he lay beneath my chair, and it is from there that I must have had him come out and sit up and beg. He sat up and begged admirably, without ever needing to be coaxed; and, when he had gotten his piece of meat or lump of sugar, he would quietly return under my seat. When I left the table, he would sometimes linger behind in the dining room, no doubt on the lookout for a little treat, or at the very least a caress; but he never got anything; people paid him no attention, which must have made him sad. So he lingered a little longer, and I had to call him several times for him to make up his mind and leave the room; dashing between my legs, he went to frisk about in the garden, through the flowers, by way of consolation. He was a charming companion, full of goodwill! Never difficult; probably faithful as well, but he never had to bare his teeth, for we never had any dangerous encounters in the course of our hikes; nor would he ever appear tired, although these walks were sometimes very long; one day we even had to return by car, so far had I wandered from my base. Was it on that day that I had gotten lost? It was then, in any case, that we had the most encounters, first with a very melancholic rider dressed in black, then with a gloomy country-man, in boots, who put us back on the right path. It was indeed that day that I lost my way. In the twilight, the sails of the windmills were turning for no other reason than to liven up the scenery. It was dark when we arrived at the hotel. Dino had kept so quiet that I even wondered whether he hadn't been running behind the car the whole time, preferring to let me enjoy in solitude the pleasantness of this means of transportation and of the beauties of the dying day. I was not at all surprised by this thoughtfulness, given his remarkable intelligence. And although this sacrifice of his was surely disinterested, he was entitled to two lumps of sugar that evening.

But it was in the direction of Cintra that I always preferred to go. The two of us, my dog and I, we had a soft spot for this road on the hill across a solitude of forests and abandoned castles where we never passed pedestrian or car. There was a convent at the bottom of a deep valley. Some coach was doubtless passing through tall, rusty gates that periwigged footmen no longer opened. Sometimes Dino and I would feel one pass near us, hazy like the vapor of winter breath, and blur behind us, erased from an uncertain world by our caprice and our fear.

Then we would arrive at Cintra with its three tiered castles. There I tasted the pleasures of archeology and Dino sniffed out the last traces of Lord Byron's insolent aroma. While I lingered before the ropes intertwined around the windows, abandoned by navigators now no longer esteemed, my dog would piss on gigantic ferns, the likes of which are not to be found elsewhere in Europe. We would finish by going together into an English-looking teahouse, whose macaroons were excellent, and return along the sea thanks to a little tram that rolled noisily along for a short hour. In the evening, the pounding of the waves at the cliffs of this Far West briefly revived the seignorial and scholarly sailors who had ventured along the African coasts, now quite dead, dead like the English lords who had come to cultivate, in the shadow of a baroque architecture, the last flowers of their eccentricity. As for myself, during the day, no less indistinct, I read the *Enneads* and painted gouaches in which the skin of a scarecrow-cat immobilized itself in its oscillation, in which undefined human forms were fixed, pinned and dying.

I stayed for two months in this village, then I had to go back to France. I was awaited near Marseilles. I returned to Lisbon and visited, one after the other, the navigation companies. There is no regular route between these two ports. I eventually discovered an empty liner, back from America, which would be putting in at Palermo and Naples. I reserved a cabin. We were to embark on Friday. In the meantime I wanted to visit Porto and Coimbra, and Dino too visited these two cities. The day before departure we were wandering about in Coimbra, and, having found the countryside, we did not return until dusk. A beautiful Mercedes was gleaming in front of the hotel; the navigation company had telephoned during our absence: the liner was leaving a day earlier than expected. We went back, swept along by a disinterested fervor. Yet we arrived too late. The liner, going up the Tagus, had already disappeared without waiting for us. I stayed there, at the edge of the quay, uncertain. What should I do? I now had to return by train, to traverse all of Spain. I was awaited near Marseilles. A wonderful chance had just been lost. Behind me, I sensed the driver sympathize with my anxiety. Then I heard something fall with a clap, then a splashing. Little by little, the noise grew fainter, and at each reflected light, the water could be seen rippling with the passage of an invisible swimming. Then nothing more could be heard; over there, the surface of light was still rippling, inexplicably; then again further off, over there; and then still further, and that was all.

Dino had left, leaving me with my dreams, abandoning me, the infidel, to the plain reality of a reserved seat on a great European express train.

1

At the forest's edge, the two companions parted. One took the path on the right, the other veered to the left, in the direction of the village. The trees thinned out, the countryside loomed up on both sides of the road, the houses drew near. The traveler, now alone, arrived like the dusk, and the lamps had just lit up in the inn when he entered the room of the cafe. Then it began to rain; and as for him, he sat down, after taking off his knapsack.

The maidservant, approaching, inquired as to his wishes. He thought of his companion, now lost in the mist. He replied: a vermouth, but I would also like a room for the night. The owner takes care of that, he's told, the owner'll come soon, you'll have to wait for him, but don't worry, you'll get a room.

The owner came, at about half a glass. The maidservant, seated in the distance, was reading a tiny novel. The traveler was thinking: where was his companion? Very damp? Or did he take refuge in a hut, a cellar, a cabin, a shelter. Or maybe he was walking between the raindrops, dry and clean.

The owner then said:

"You want a room, monsieur?"

"Yes, for the night."

"Nothing easier, tourists are rare this time of year, you can choose the nicest room."

"No doubt, but . . . the price?"

"The room's twenty francs, monsieur, and I told you: you can choose the nicest room, the one I rent for fifty in the summer. You can take the one you like the most. A guest is, for me, monsieur, an individual who has rights, I'll go even better, monsieur," said the innkeeper, "for me a guest is an individual whom I respect."

"You surprise me," said the traveler, "that's unusual for your trade."

"Monsieur, monsieur, don't criticize the profession. I know that I'm an exception, but even so, monsieur, solidarity, monsieur."

"I didn't mean to offend you."

"You couldn't if you wanted, monsieur, since, I repeat, for me a guest is, so to speak, how shall I say it, in a word, sacred."

"Gosh," said the traveler.

And he looked at the innkeeper.

A larded fellow, clean-shaven, pinkish, of respectable height. He held his hands on his thighs and was looking beyond his walls; he filled the room, but worried about extreme edges. He said:

"Let's say that I'm not like the others."

And smiled.

"Let's say," said the traveler, "that I'll take the best room and for twenty francs, to please you."

"You've never been here before?" asked the innkeeper.

"No. I didn't even know Saint-Certain-sur-Chrêche existed until yesterday. I'm going to Gougougnac and I'm coming from Cougorge."

"At this time of year?"

"I take my vacation this time of year. There's a very beautiful church at Gougougnac, isn't there?"

"So they say, monsieur. I have to go now. Take number 1, then. Hortense, prepare number 1 for monsieur."

He murmured:

"It's strange, it's still not him."

The traveler watched him disappear. As Hortense had obeyed on the spot, he found himself alone and remained so for a very long time, before his glass which he was emptying with short gulps, near the window beaten by the gusts of rain. An automobile passed, splashing. Another. But there was nothing in particular to see; and the ground of the deserted road soaked under the observer's eyes.

After an indeterminate length of time, the owner returned, a sheet of paper in his hand, and asked the traveler if he would mind filling out the guest history card: which was done.

Alone again, the traveler continued to gaze at the rain or around him at the room. Then it was night. So it was the maid's turn to reappear. She turned on two or three switches and the cafe was lit up. This task accomplished, she left again.

The traveler remained alone again for a certain amount of time; resounding pellets of water were running along the windowpanes. His glass was now empty. He looked around him.

One of the doors that opened into the cafe was, at a certain given moment, pushed open; the traveler saw no one enter; he leaned over the table, investigating, and saw a dog which had just entered.

The dog, definitely a mongrel, looking somewhat like a fox terrier and with a rather brown coat, inspected the legs of two or three tables or chairs, sniffing, turned two or three times in a circle,[1] then, in a discrete manner, approached the newcomer indirectly. The latter was making little whistling noises with his mouth, a way of coaxing the animal, which, with a sure and supple movement, leapt onto the chair opposite the traveler and sat there.

Both looked at one another.

"You'd like a lump of sugar, eh, my little dog," said the traveler.

"I am not *your* dog," replied the quadruped. "I belong to no one but myself. And I'm not the house dog, either; if the proprietor of this establishment imagines so, he is very much mistaken. As for the sugar, I'm quite fond of it, and would not be averse to a piece. Ah, over there, on the chest of drawers, there's a full sugar bowl; if it wouldn't be any trouble, I would be much obliged if you got me one."

The traveler remained motionless and silent for a moment, yet without the features of his face displaying any marks of surprise or terror. He soon rose, went to find a lump of sugar, and offered it to the dog, who munched it.

After licking his chops, the dog said:

"I'm called Dino. That's my name: Dino."

"Delighted," said the traveler. "I'm Amédée Gubernatis, the youngest deputy of France."[2]

"Very honored," said the dog. "You're of Italian origin?"

"As are many good Frenchmen," replied the deputy.

"Don't be offended, please, Monsieur Amédée," said the dog, "I'm not in the least racist, although I can lay claim to a high pedigree on my father's side."

He smiled and, serious, added:

"You must be bored here."

"Me? Not at all," said Amédée. "Anyway, I'm never bored."

"Only animals are never bored," said the dog, "or individuals not far removed from the natural life. But coming from a deputy, that would surprise me."

"I've always some project in my head," said Amédée, "some plan, some construction, law, decree."

"You must be overworked," said the dog, shaking his head.

"What's that, overworked? Certainly, since the age of thirteen, I've never ceased to work, and from twelve to sixteen hours a day."

"You give me the creeps," said the dog. "Would it be a nuisance if I asked you to go get me another lump of sugar?"

"It would be my pleasure," said Amédée.

The lump of sugar munched, the conversation resumed.

"Why work so much?" asked the dog.

"I'm a specialist. A specialist in budgetary and financial questions. I'm not only a doctor in law and holder of a diploma in poli sci, I'm also a doctor in science. That's never been heard of; it's also my strength . . . one of my strengths."

"You're an ambitious man," said the dog, finishing licking his chops.

"An ambitious man . . . an ambitious man . . . that's easier said than done . . . an ambitious man . . ."

"Do you think of the good of the people? Of your citizens?"

"Certainly. It's for them that I became a specialist. After all, not everyone can be as learned as I: it's for their good that I'm accumulating so much power. I'm struggling for them thanks to these arms."

"Hmph," went the dog. "Hmph."

"Let's say then that I'm an ambitious man," granted Amédée. "For the time being, I'm on vacation."

"Alone?"

"Just recently. I left a fellow traveler. I'm traveling by foot across this region. It's very instructive. And what memories!"

The dog yawned and leapt down from his chair. He made two or three turns, sniffed two or three things, and left, pushing open another door, without having uttered a farewell. Almost immediately, through an entrance, the maid appeared who asked Gubernatis if he would be having dinner.

He would be having dinner.

What?

Being the only traveler, they were only able to feed him the basics.

But Gubernatis was not a gourmet.

The maid put a tablecloth before him, garnished it; and some time after, came back with a tureen. The meal consisted of soup, an omelet, a salad and a piece of fruit. All of it was expressly served and consumed no less rapidly. The maid rubbed a bit against the customer, but he took no interest, at least, no visible interest. A little before the traveler had finished peeling his apple, a one-eyed old man in velvet trousers entered.

"Hortense, a very hot picon," he announced very loudly.

He looked at the traveler from his only porthole.

"So how's it going, Monsieur Blandi," said the maidservant, "same as always, you clumsy old clot."

The traveler realized that the new arrival was deaf. The maidservant served the picon with hot water, then stayed there rubbing a thigh.

"It's going alright, Hortense," resumed the one-eyed old man. "Though there's my rheumama. Bah, it's nothing. It's nothing. The rain, today, um! The snails are coming out."

He looked at the traveler.

"This is no weather for walking," he affirmed. "You've no luck with an atmosphere like this."

Although this sentence was addressed, obviously, to him, the traveler didn't reply.

"The mushrooms are going to rot," resumed the one-eyed man, "and the grapes aren't going to be good, no sir. Rotten mushrooroos, stripped vine, that's what I reckon."

"Ah, clumsy old clot," said Hortense, smiling.

She pulled on her girdle, which was rolling up over her buttocks. She stayed planted there. The traveler had finished his fruit.

"Coffee?"

"No thank you."

"That keeps you from sleeping," said the old man.

"Mind your own business, you old smock," said Hortense and, addressing the traveler: "He's my uncle. He's gaga."

"Says her," replied the one-eyed man, who was not the slightest bit deaf. "Says her. If it wasn't for my rheumama, I'd be fit as a fiddle. As a fiddle."

"He's a little screwy," said Hortense. "He still tinkers about in spite of his age. There's some that take him for a sorcerer. He puts bones back into place, you know, and puts spells on fire. He knows all the plants by their names, and what they can be used for. They even used to say that in the past he conjured up the dead."

"Nonsense," said the one-eyed man.

"There's a talking head at his house that tells him everything that goes on in the world," continued Hortense as she cleared the table— and doing this she took advantage of every chance to press her hard breast against the other man's shoulder or to rub her thigh against his arm—"no one's ever seen it, except me once when I was little, I was so scared, there're people who say it's a radio, even so, the proof's that when I was little radios didn't exist—because I'm not old, monsieur, I'm twenty; so they tell me that I dreamed it. All the same, I saw that head, I did."

"By chance," said the one-eyed man.

"He also has two crows which spy for him, they fly all over the place, land on windowsills, look, and then they repeat what they've seen. Sometimes the young guys from around here try to kill them, but they never succeed, on the contrary: they either injure themselves or else they break something."

"Quite right," said the one-eyed man.

Hortense made a gesture:

"He's the only one in my family like that."

The traveler lit a pipe.

"You're taking a trip on foot, monsieur," the old man said to him. "You find out a lot more that way than with the rayrailroads or the automotos. You see things that speed doesn't let you, right?"

"That's right."

"You're spending the night here?"

"Yes."

"Then come see me tomorrow morning at my home, I'll show you some interesting things. You're a scholar, in numbers, eh, statistiti?"

"How do you know that?"

"Hortense told you, one of my crows saw you come, and you were mumbling nunumbers half-aloud, half-low."

The traveler smiled:

"It's a habit I should break."

"Come see me tomorrow, then," resumed the one-eyed man, getting up. "The picon, it's on monsieur," he added.

And he left.

"Old cheapo," murmured Hortense, "and completely off his rocker, completely. But it's true that I saw his talking head, when I was little."

There was a silence.

"I'll take you to your room," said Hortense.

The traveler was getting up to follow her when the owner entered.

"How was dinner, Monsieur Gubernatis? You can go to bed when you've finished the dishes. How was dinner, Monsieur Gubernatis? It's difficult for me to cook at this time of year, given the small number, the minute number even, I dare say, of customers; also given that I don't know how to cook—an omelet's not cooking. I thus have neither provisions nor cooks. Anyway, how was dinner, Monsieur Gubernatis?"

"Quite good. I'm not a big eater."

"Ah ah! There's reproach behind that sentence."

"Not at all. I dined very well."

"My little omelet was a success?"

"Excellent."

"Hm."

He stared hard at the traveler.

"If I read your card right, you're indeed Monsieur Gubernatis?"

"In person. You have your doubts?"

"Not at all. Not at all. The deputy?"

"Yes."

"My house is honored by your visit, Monsieur Deputy. And . . . but . . . another thing: you've never been here before?"

"Never."

"You're sure?"

"Without a doubt. Absolutely sure."

"You've never been here before?"

"I told you, never."

"Not even in a dream?"

Gubernatis thought it over.

"Not even in a dream," he replied.

He remarked:

"Strange interrogation."

The chubby-cheeked fellow who had asked his questions with a mask of anxiety recovered an affable appearance.

"I'm sorry, Monsieur Deputy, I'm sorry. I'm a little excessive on this matter. It would be a long story to tell you, a long story."

He directed a slightly imploring eye at his customer, as if he had wanted this customer to beseech him to tell the story. But this customer, perhaps already tired from too many (autobiographical) stories already recounted in one evening, answered simply:

"Everyone has a story to tell."

This reply seemed to stun the fellow who was overcome by a somewhat hypomanic nervousness.

"Ex-," he said, "-cuse me, Monsieur Deputy, excuse me, my story is not at all like that of others, not at all. First off it has nothing extraordinary about it my story, primo. And secundimo, it's not ordinary."

At this moment one of the doors which gave onto the cafe opened silently and Gubernatis saw the dog appear. He wandered about in a circle for several seconds, then, with a supple and determined leap, climbed up onto a chair between the innkeeper and the traveler, and sat down.

"He's yours, the dog?" asked Amédée.

The innkeeper looked sideways, in the direction of the animal, as if to make sure.

"Yes. His name's Dino."

"He must have a story, too," said Gubernatis.

He looked at the dog, but the dog pretended he didn't understand and closed his eyes and yawned, then resumed his impassivity.

"He's a good little doggie," said the innkeeper distractedly. "My story, Monsieur Deputy . . ."

"Tell it to me then."

"It's simple, it's short, it's clear. Here it is. My name, Monsieur Deputy, is Raphaël Desnouettes.[3] My father was in the hotel business, my grandfather was a cook, my great grandfather, Monsieur Deputy, even wrote a book on the presentation of dishes—you see what sort of artisanal, as it were, aristocracy we represent. I don't say that to offend you, Monsieur Deputy, I know you're a radical-socialist. Good, I was telling you, then, that having been born into the trade, I was raised in it, I was fed up with it: I wanted to be a sailor, monsieur. I was actually an apprentice in the Merchant Service. When my father died, though, I felt it was my duty to go back into the trade, if only to console my mother in her old age, a chambermaid who respected our family traditions. So I settled here, ten years ago. My mother died two years later. I was thus an orphan, you'll notice. I'm coming to my story. I'd been set up here for five years already—this is thus five years ago, you'll notice, Monsieur Deputy— when, on a day similar to this one, a traveler entered who, like yourself, was making his way on foot. He was a rather tall man, certainly an athlete, with a very handsome face, Monsieur Deputy, and eyes—eyes—eyes of unusual brilliance. He stayed an hour, enough time to drink a bottle of red wine. What he talked about, because I went over to make conversation with him, I can no longer recall. That's what I can no longer recall," he groaned. "He had been gone for maybe ten minutes, when I realized that I had just been paid a visit—by an ape."

"An ape?" asked Gubernatis.

The dog closed his eyes and tilted his head to one side.

"I know that I'm going against your innermost sentiments, Monsieur Deputy," said Desnouettes.

"Not at all, not at all," murmured Gubernatis.

"Yes, yes, I know I am. An ape! An ape! Nevertheless, yes, it was an ape who had honored me with his visit and since that day I've been waiting for his return, and every guest is for me as it were—honorable, respected! Yourself, Monsieur Deputy, you most particularly, you among others, aren't you a bit like the one who must return here?"

"Are you sure that he'll return?"

The hotelier smiled with a knowing air:

"Certain, Monsieur Deputy, certain."

The dog reopened his eyes.

"On the one hand," asked Gubernatis, "you seem to be very sure of his appearance, but on the other, you appear anxious to find him in anyone. I mean: me, for example, I don't think I look anything like your ape and yet you questioned me as if I might have indeed been him."

"Yes. But no contradiction, Monsieur Deputy: I simply think that he can alter his appearance, that he can take on another form."

"But how would you recognize him, then?"

"By a sign. Of some sort."

"And you can't remember anything that he said to you."

"Nothing. And yet since then I've often thought about it. But nothing. Nothing."

Then:

"You'll agree to an old calva. I have some that's excellent. I'll go get it."

He rushed off.

As soon as he had passed to the other side of the door, the dog said:

"What do you think of the owner's story?"

"Not much. I'm not in the habit of talking like this. I'm only familiar with more precise notions."

"Yes, the owner's a dreamer, isn't he?"

"Him a dreamer, me an ambitious man, you label men pretty quickly, Monsieur Dino. And you, what are you then?"

"A dog."

But as the owner was reappearing, Dino didn't say anything more.

The calvados was quite strong, and Gubernatis made the customary compliments to the hotelier; and the hotelier gathered them without the least amount of pride or the least amount of modesty. He remained as quiet as his dog. He seemed to have lost all desire to tell his stories.

In the deserted street, an approaching step was heard and soon the door began to open. Dino leapt down from his chair and went to bark. A head passed through the opening, that of the one-eyed old man.

"You'll come by to see me tomorrow morning, Monsieur Traveler," said the head.

"Count on it."

"Good night."

The head disappeared and the door shut again. Dino had already gotten back onto his chair.

"You already know him?" asked Desnouettes.

"He was just here a short while ago. But—who is he exactly?"

"How do I know? Who knows? He's an old lunatic, that's all."

The dog gave the traveler a sidelong glance and smiled. Then yawned, got off of his chair, moving away with a sure step to the swinging door he pushed open, and disappeared in his turn.

They heard steps above their heads.

"The maid's getting your room ready," said the hotelier.

"I heard some odd things about this one-eyed man."

"From whom?"

"Your maid."

The hotelier shrugged his shoulders.

"Bah, they're superstitious in this godforsaken place. Gossip. Stupid sometimes. Some of them go so far as to say that my dog talks."

Gubernatis began to laugh: well, that's a bit much!

"And that he can even make himself invisible."

"In other times they would have burned him and you along with."

"Me? Me? But, Monsieur Deputy, I'm a pure-hearted man. What do I have to do with such foolishness?"

"They would have also burned that one-eyed old man."

"A madman! He's a madman!"

"Nowadays they no longer burn madmen at the stake."

"No."

The hotelier got quiet and became silent again. Above their heads it got quiet and the glasses were emptied.

"I'm going to go to bed," said Gubernatis, getting up. "Thank you for the excellent calva."

He took his knapsack.

"You'll find your room?" said Desnouettes, without getting up. "It's just across from the staircase. It's number 1."

"Good night, Monsieur Desnouettes."

"Good night, Monsieur Deputy."

But he didn't get up.

Gubernatis pushed the door open; the staircase was still lit; under the steps he saw, lying on some rags, Dino, who was sleeping. He went up softly, the wood creaked, the dog didn't wake up.

He entered his room and, in the bed, there, naturally, was Hortense.

II

The next morning Amédée woke up, refreshed and full of energy, to the first rays of the sun. He performed his daily and methodical gymnastics, carried out his ablutions, and got dressed. Then went down. Into the common room, his bag already ready, and he to leave.

"What would monsieur like?" asked Hortense at the kitchen exit.

"Black coffee, bread, butter, jam."

Outside, some people were active in the rustic morning, horses as well, cars, tipcarts, harrows; cats, dogs; children; all with discretion, even if with cries. His coffee, with bread-butter-jam, was served to him; he absorbed it with delight and pleasure, alone at first, for Hortense, unkempt at that time of the morning, had fled to the kitchens, then with the company of Dino, who, the door closed, had leapt onto a chair across from him. He offered him a lump of sugar.

"With pleasure," said the dog, who began to munch.

"Beautiful weather this morning," said Amédée.

"Quite," said the dog, licking his chops still covered with sugar.

"I'm going to have lovely weather for my next leg," said Amédée.

"The weather can change," said the dog.

"Between now and this afternoon?"

"The weather's never certain around here. You're going to see the uncle."

"Ah yes, that's right! Probably. Anyway, I didn't forget him."

"And Hortense?"

"I turned her out. She was in my bed!"

"It's true, you turned her out. She's very offended."

"You don't think I'm going to botch my entire career for an amorous adventure with a servant?"

"More than one politician has had mistresses . . . adventures . . . and good fortune."

"Ugh. I'm not the type. I have nothing I can be reproached for, neither from that point of view, nor from the business point of view. That's my strength . . . one of the aspects of my strength; my knowledge is the other aspect."

"Are you really so strong?" asked the dog. "You've never been a minister, as far as I know."

"Wait a bit. And anyway one can be strong without having to cry it out from the rooftops."

"Would you be a freemason?"

"Bah. A strength, true, but one which is fading. Anyway, I actually am a F ∴ M ∴."[4]

"Has that been of any use to you?"

"Not much. I'd rather learn the secrets of others than disguise myself in secret."

"That somewhat contradicts what you were asserting just now."

"Not at all, not at all. Think about it."

The deputy looked at the dog with fondness.

"I like you," he said, "and I would very much like to have the pleasure of your company. I would buy you from Monsieur Desnouettes if I weren't afraid that once bought you would stop talking."

"What makes you think so?"

"In any case, I know that dogs don't talk. There's probably a microphone system under this table, and the real person I'm speaking to is in the next room. He's listening to me, he replies to me. I'll take advantage of this situation, moreover, to tell him that I would be happy to make his acquaintance in flesh and blood."

"Well!" went the dog, "that's really something. You see a dog talking and you don't believe it?"

"You're well-trained, that's all."

"Well, well—and if I told you that I had still other talents."

"Which are?"

"For example, I can make myself invisible."

"Show me."

"But first tell me how this night with Hortense went."

"Very simply. I asked her to leave. She thought I was joking. But she eventually understood. She left. I deeply regret humiliating her like that, but what do you expect—my destiny . . ."

"Yes, yes," went the dog pensively.

"You're rather interested in this person?"

"We were very close," said the dog modestly, lowering his head.

"Ah, ah," went Amédée, discreetly.

They remained silent.

"And this invisibility?" asked the traveler.

"Ah yes, this invisibility. Well, do you want it to be progressive and continuous, or abrupt and sudden?"

"Well . . ."

"As you like."

"Let's say progressive and continuous."

Dino immediately leapt down from his chair and began to describe the largest circle he could possibly trace in the middle of the room without running into a chair. Coming near his starting point, he tilted his body while walking, he traced a second circle of a slightly smaller radius at the same time as his own dimensions reduced themselves proportionally, and describing in this way a spiral, he ended up being no more than a kind of tiny canine atom turning with an ever increasing speed about the usual axis of symmetry of the geometrical figure thus suggested; and finally, through a passage to the limit, this vibrio, attaining dimensions of such indefinite smallness, ended up disappearing.

"Quite a trick," murmured the traveler. "But I've seen even better magicians. Darn, there I am talking to myself again; I need to break that lousy habit."

He went to leave his knapsack near the cash desk, not wanting to bother anyone, and left. Outside, a nice humid warmth fingered his sense of smell; feeling lively, he set out to find the dwelling of the one-eyed uncle; and was not at all long in finding it.

. . . .

One plus one act to precede a drama

Characters

IRÈNE	SABINE
JOACHIM	ÉTIENNE
MALE PASSERBY	MALE BEGGAR
FEMALE BEGGAR	FEMALE PASSERBY

A metro corridor. A female beggar, standing against the back wall, holds out her hand. A male passerby gives her twenty sous.

FEMALE BEGGAR, *unpleasantly.*

Thanks for the leftovers, my good fellow.

MALE PASSERBY

I'm sorry! I didn't mean to offend you.

FEMALE BEGGAR

No harm done.

MALE PASSERBY

What do you expect! I was only passing by.

He leaves. He will return. It will always be the same male passerby. He will simply change his headgear. This time, for example, he is wearing a soft fedora.
A period of time passes.
Enter a lady and a gentleman with a heavy suitcase.

IRÈNE, *stopping, exhausted.*

That's it.

JOACHIM, *setting down his suitcase.*

I've had it.

IRÈNE, *contemptuously.*

Had what?

JOACHIM

I'm telling you, I've had it. There must be fifty pounds of feathers in this van of yours. What did you put in it?

IRÈNE

That's hardly the problem!

JOACHIM

What's the problem, then?

IRÈNE

You're asking me?

JOACHIM

So it seems.

IRÈNE

I'm tired.

JOACHIM

So am I.

MALE PASSERBY *enters. He's wearing the cocked hat of an employee of the Bank of France. Three quarters of the way across, he stops and says amiably.*

How much I'm taking today . . . but I'm only passing by.

He leaves.

IRÈNE, *to Joachim.*

Do you love me?

JOACHIM

As if this was any place to ask a question like that. I even have a vague feeling that there's a draft.

IRÈNE, *very serious.*

Do you love me?

JOACHIM

I really wonder what you could have crammed into this thing. *(He weighs up the suitcase.)* I can't go on. *(He puts the suitcase back down.)*

IRÈNE, *even more serious.*

Do you love me?

JOACHIM

Yes, of course. Thank god it's sturdy, otherwise everything in it would clear out onto the floor.

IRÈNE

I wonder if you love me.

JOACHIM

I'm glad you lost the other one, you know, that pigskin suitcase, because I wouldn't have been able to even drag that one this far.

IRÈNE

Sometimes I look at you and it seems like I'm seeing through you, as if you no longer existed for me.

JOACHIM

I can understand that. Right now, for instance, I feel like I'm completely transparent. I'm so tired I'm empty.

IRÈNE

Deep down you don't love me.

JOACHIM

But I do, I do. Just let me rest a bit after making an effort like that.

MALE PASSERBY *comes in again. Top hat. He looks as if he's in a hurry. To female beggar.*

No time to search my pockets. I'll get you next time.

FEMALE BEGGAR

You're too kind, my good sir.

MALE PASSERBY

You understand, I'm only passing by. *(He leaves.)*

IRÈNE, *great sigh.*

JOACHIM

What's up? You not feeling well? That should be me. It's a real job lugging your wardrobe, you know.

IRÈNE

I want you to listen to me. I've something serious to tell you.

JOACHIM

Here?

IRÈNE

Here.

44

JOACHIM

Here? With the suitcase, the beggar, and the draft?

IRÈNE

Yes.

JOACHIM, *he sits down on the suitcase.*

I'm listening.

IRÈNE

You don't love me.

JOACHIM

Is that an assertion, question or negation?

IRÈNE

You don't love me. It's obvious.

JOACHIM, *getting up abruptly.*

Good heavens! It's obvious? How's that?

IRÈNE

No, you don't love me! You don't love me! You don't love me! *(She gets worked up and wants to cry.)* You're an uncut stone, a rock, a buffoon, a shovel resting in the corner, a sidewalk corner, a page of arithmetic with little doodles on top, but you're not a lover.

> *The male passerby enters. Cap. Hands in pockets, he is whistling a tune that's in fashion. Passes. And exits.*

IRÈNE

Life with you is becoming incredibly boring. You overwhelm me with your grayness and it's cold being with you. *(Joachim takes the suitcase and carries it—just barely—over to the female beggar. He sits down on it and stays there, an attentive listener.)* I'm dying of cold! I'm dying of boredom! Ah! Any man would be warmer than you! Say something, won't you.

JOACHIM

What do you want me to say?

IRÈNE

You're a brute. *(Silence.)*

IRÈNE

Any man would be more loving, more passionate . . .

JOACHIM

That's some imagination you have.

FEMALE BEGGAR

We women are never short of imagination.

JOACHIM

No one asked you for your opinion.

IRÈNE

Any man . . .

JOACHIM, *putting his head in his hands.*

You're becoming more tiresome than the suitcase.

IRÈNE

Any man . . .

Enter the male passerby, head bare.

IRÈNE

Hey!

The male passerby stops.

IRÈNE

Passerby!

The male passerby points to himself questioningly.
Irène nods her head affirmatively.
The male passerby approaches.

IRÈNE

Monsieur . . . uh . . . could you tell me the time?

MALE PASSERBY, *he looks at his wristwatch.*

It's 4:35.

JOACHIM, *sitting on the suitcase.*

Really?

MALE PASSERBY, *to Irène.*

I must say that that doesn't sound right. *(He looks at his watch carefully.)* Yet that's what it is.

IRÈNE, *also looking.*

MALE PASSERBY

Yes. 4:35.

JOACHIM, *sitting on his suitcase.*

It's not possible.

MALE PASSERBY, *to Irène.*

Really?

IRÈNE

Maybe your watch stopped.

The male passerby brings his watch to his ear. He listens carefully.

FEMALE BEGGAR

Tick tock, tick tock, tick tock.

MALE PASSERBY

All the same, it seems to be working.

IRÈNE

No, that's the echo.

MALE PASSERBY

Really? *(He listens.)*

FEMALE BEGGAR

Tick tock, tick tock, tick tock.

IRÈNE

You know how it is . . . The way we see the light of stars that have been dead for millions of years . . .

The male passerby listens again to his watch.

FEMALE BEGGAR *remains silent.*

MALE PASSERBY

You're right. It stopped.

IRÈNE

Too bad.

MALE PASSERBY

I can get the time from this gentleman.

IRÈNE

Don't bother. That's my husband.

MALE PASSERBY

And he doesn't have a watch?

IRÈNE

He does.

MALE PASSERBY

It isn't working either?

IRÈNE

I don't want to know.

MALE PASSERBY

You don't want me to ask him?

IRÈNE

Please . . . don't.

MALE PASSERBY

Very well . . . I'm only too happy to be able to comply with one of your wishes and, as I'm extremely sorry to be unable to furnish you with the information you requested, would you please accept, madame, my devoted and good wishes. *(He bows.)*

Irène also bows.

The male passerby makes a show of moving away.

IRÈNE, *holding him back.*

Monsieur.

MALE PASSERBY, *returning immediately.*

Madame?

IRÈNE

This watch . . .

MALE PASSERBY

Yes? . . .

IRÈNE

It's nice.

MALE PASSERBY

Really?

IRÈNE

Yes, elegant even.

MALE PASSERBY

It's square.

IRÈNE

Style doesn't always come in round packages.

MALE PASSERBY

That's what I've always vaguely thought.

IRÈNE

You've had it a long time?

MALE PASSERBY

Let's see *(he reflects)* . . . For some time now already . . . *(He reflects again.)* But now . . . How should I know!

IRÈNE

It was a present?

MALE PASSERBY

Yes.

IRÈNE

From your wife?

MALE PASSERBY

No.

IRÈNE

You're married?

MALE PASSERBY *moves back two steps in order to examine Irène—especially her legs: Irène must wear a very short skirt. On reflection.*

No.

He draws near. A period of time passes.

IRÈNE

A girlfriend?

MALE PASSERBY

No.

IRÈNE, *lively.*

A family keepsake?

MALE PASSERBY

No *(with decision.)* A present from my masseur.

IRÈNE

I would very much like to know the make.

MALE PASSERBY, *examining his watch.*

It says *Electra*. It must be that.

IRÈNE

Swiss?

MALE PASSERBY

I don't see the little flag.

IRÈNE

Doesn't matter.

MALE PASSERBY

You're not particularly attached to it being Swiss?

IRÈNE

No, not at all.

MALE PASSERBY

In any case, it isn't working anymore.

IRÈNE

Perhaps you forgot to rewind it.

The male passerby turns the winder indefinitely.

FEMALE BEGGAR

That bothers some people, a watch that doesn't work.

JOACHIM

Some even get irritated. They end up grinding their teeth and then, of course, it makes them late.

MALE PASSERBY, *tired of turning the winder.*

The mechanism seems to be busted. Anyway, I can't remember anymore if it ever worked. I never looked at it. If you hadn't drawn my attention to it . . .

IRÈNE, *in a very conventional tone.*

All the same, a watch can be very useful.

MALE PASSERBY

Yes. It's used to measure time.

IRÈNE

Which isn't easy.

MALE PASSERBY, *also very conventional.*

I've heard that there are watches that give the days of the week, the months, even the years.

FEMALE BEGGAR, *to Joachim.*

I've seen some like that at the flea market.

JOACHIM

Will you take me there?

IRÈNE, *to the male passerby.*

We'll go together, if you like. You can find charming things there.

MALE PASSERBY

And such weird things. One time I found a little scrap of paper there. Yes. A little scrap of paper. That was it *(dreamy).* Strange, isn't it? *(Abruptly.)* But . . . you did say "we'll go together" a second ago?

IRÈNE

Yes, I just said "we'll go together."

FEMALE BEGGAR

Tonight's too late.

JOACHIM

Of course.

MALE PASSERBY

So, we should arrange to meet?

IRÈNE

No?

MALE PASSERBY, *bowing.*

I would be delighted.

IRÈNE

People generally go there on Sundays.

MALE PASSERBY

And what day is this?

IRÈNE

Thursday.

FEMALE BEGGAR

Friday.

JOACHIM

Saturday.

MALE PASSERBY, *he looks up.*

I'm not too bright when it comes to astronomy . . . *(Lively:)* You like the stars?

IRÈNE, *with modesty.*

Oh yes.

MALE PASSERBY

We're going to get along so well!

IRÈNE   •

Sometimes I look at them so insistently that I'm overcome by vertigo and I have the impression that I'm going to fall into the sky.

MALE PASSERBY

Which after all is only a big hole, a sort of pit, an abyss like the others.

IRÈNE

But . . . you did say just now: "We're going to get along so well."

MALE PASSERBY

Yes. I just said: "We're going to get along so well."

IRÈNE, *dreamily.*

We . . .

MALE PASSERBY

Yes: we.

IRÈNE

We, and the stars.

MALE PASSERBY

That makes a lot. They're numerous.

IRÈNE

Hundreds.

MALE PASSERBY

Thousands.

JOACHIM

Millions.

FEMALE BEGGAR

Billions.

IRÈNE

You think?

MALE PASSERBY

There are specialists who say so. But what interests me is their disorder.

IRÈNE

They were thrown into space like dice on a green cloth.

MALE PASSERBY

And no one's won.

FEMALE BEGGAR

They're never going to get there.

Silence. The female beggar shakes Joachim who was asleep.

JOACHIM

Where are they at?

FEMALE BEGGAR

They're a little lost.

JOACHIM

Already?

IRÈNE, *resuming the conversation, again very conventional.*

You're a gambler, monsieur?

MALE PASSERBY

Bah! I like a little belote from time to time.

IRÈNE

I love poker.

MALE PASSERBY, *barefacedly lying.*

Me too.

IRÈNE

Really?

MALE PASSERBY

Yes. And I bet that you like to cheat.

IRÈNE

Yes.

MALE PASSERBY

We'll get along perfectly: me too.

JOACHIM

Let's sum up: Visit to the flea market in the morning, a bit of shifty-eyed poker in the evening, contemplation of the starry sky after midnight, most of the time's already accounted for. But they still don't know what to do with their afternoon.

FEMALE BEGGAR

They could go for a walk.

IRÈNE

If he wants.

JOACHIM

They could go to the movies.

MALE PASSERBY

If she wants.

JOACHIM *and* FEMALE BEGGAR, *in chorus.*

What do they want?

IRÈNE *and* MALE PASSERBY, *in chorus.*

To go for a walk.

IRÈNE

Yes, that's it.

MALE PASSERBY

We'll take the metro.

IRÈNE

A Sunday afternoon. We'll jostle with the parents who are going to show the grandmothers to the unhappy grandkids.

MALE PASSERBY

We'll go first class. I'm paying.

IRÈNE

We'll go past all the stations. We won't get off until the terminus.

MALE PASSERBY

And there we have to put our feet on the ground. We shoot up to the surface. We look around us.

IRÈNE

What do we see? Already . . . the outer boulevards of Paris . . . the fortifications . . .

MALE PASSERBY

The grass is growing on the embankments . . . Citizens are resting; they bare their chests to the sun, vests unbuttoned.

IRÈNE

Girls with big chignons have little red aprons.

MALE PASSERBY

Down there, near the tollhouse, the local trains depart, pulled by fiery chargers.

IRÈNE

Armed cavalrymen form the guard. The roads aren't safe.

MALE PASSERBY

We'll hesitate between the one painted blue, which leaves for Orléans and the one painted green, which leaves for the Atlantic.

IRÈNE

We'll take the green. The cavalrymen prance about on their horses and fire their guns into the air, in the joy of departure.

MALE PASSERBY

The countryside passes by on the right and on the left, and the villages. Soon there'll be no one else but us on the unfolding road, just us.

IRÈNE

When we arrive, on the shore, we'll bathe our horses in the sea . . .

MALE PASSERBY

In the rays of the setting sun.

IRÈNE

If some small boat passes near the shore, we'll catch up to it in a perfect crawl and the sailors will take us on.

MALE PASSERBY

On this great three-master sailing ship, leaving for the West Indies with a jazz band on board and some cases of whisky.

IRÈNE

We'll spend our days lying abaft on the rigging, and as the flying fish come soaring out of the water onto the deck, the captain, seated in front of us at a little table, will play endless games of lexicon, swearing copiously when he loses.

MALE PASSERBY

The nights will come, and the Negro musicians will beat their calabashes and blow into their brass instruments until finally the day emerges from the horizon, hauling its big, warm, red, luminous ball up out of the darkness.

IRÈNE

We'll arrive at those lands where we would never have hoped to live, with their cities larger than Paris, their avenues shaded by more palm trees than the procession of Palm Sunday, their metros of fine gold, and their silver taxis.

MALE PASSERBY

There will be fonts full of milk in the streets where the lionesses drink[1] and great frozen poles on which the snakes coil.

IRÈNE

We'll be alone amidst a joyous and colorful crowd, escorted by great shouts and harmonicas.

MALE PASSERBY

We'll dive into the pond of happiness and marinate there all day, imputrescibly.

IRÈNE

We'll relate our childhood memories and we'll have dreams, ineluctably.

MALE PASSERBY

For us, everything will have been already seen, each gesture wasted, each word a slip of the tongue—imperceptibly.

IRÈNE

Our future shall crumble in our hands and we'll stay young . . . young . . . young—incalculably.

MALE PASSERBY

There will be no more summer evenings, nor winter mornings, and our sunsets will take place at noon—improbably.

IRÈNE

We'll recapture the happy fragments of our past and we'll relive them with obstinacy—recurring eternally.

MALE PASSERBY

You shall be my winged sandal, my flying carpet, my magic language.

IRÈNE

You shall be my great unpostered wall, my port of shadows, my journey of no return . . .

MALE PASSERBY

We'll exist together.

IRÈNE

We exist together.

MALE PASSERBY, *takes her into his arms.*

I love you.

IRÈNE

I love you.

At this moment a violent ringing of bell.

FEMALE BEGGAR

Ah, they're closing down.

JOACHIM, *who had again fallen asleep.*

What's that?

FEMALE BEGGAR

The sweep.[2]

JOACHIM

The sweep?

FEMALE BEGGAR

The last metro, you twit.

She leaves. New ringing of bell. Irène and the male passerby look into each other's eyes. They don't move in the slightest. Joachim gets up, takes his suitcase and begins heading to the right. He calls.

JOACHIM

Irène!

In a very natural tone of voice, without authority, like something obvious. Irène doesn't move.

JOACHIM

Irène!

Irène doesn't move. Ringing of bell.

JOACHIM

Irène! You hear me? It's the last metro.

At these words, she jumps.

IRÈNE

What?

JOACHIM

I said it's the last metro.

IRÈNE

Ah *(to the male passerby:)* Monsieur . . . *(She extricates herself.)* Monsieur . . . I'm sorry . . . you understand . . . *(She moves away)* the last metro.

She is at Joachim's side. They leave together. On his part, the male passerby has moved away.

IRÈNE, *turning back, with a gesture of regret.*

. . . the last metro . . .

MALE PASSERBY, *with an equally regretful gesture.*

. . . What do you expect . . . I was only passing by.

They each go their separate way.

CURTAIN

Same metro corridor. A male beggar, standing against the back wall, holds out his hand. A female passerby gives him twenty sous.

MALE BEGGAR, *unpleasantly.*

Twenty sous! What do you expect me to do with twenty sous! *(Getting indignant:)* No, but really, what do you expect me to do with twenty sous!

FEMALE PASSERBY, *timidly.*

Start saving.

MALE BEGGAR

It makes me sick to hear such sophisms!

I'm sorry, I was only passing by.

She leaves. She'll come back. It will always be the same female passerby. She will simply change attire. For example, this time she is wearing some kind of hat.

Enter a gentleman and a lady. The gentleman is carrying a heavy suitcase.

SABINE

Couldn't you hurry up a bit?

ÉTIENNE, *putting down the suitcase.*

What do you expect, it's goddamn heavy.

SABINE, *contemptuously.*

Heavy? A feather!

ÉTIENNE

I'd like to see you do it.

SABINE

What do you mean, see me do it . . . As if it wasn't the man's role to carry burdens.

ÉTIENNE

I'll grant you that.

SABINE, *ironic.*

You don't have to grant me anything. That's how it is.

ÉTIENNE, *meditative.*

Yes . . . Yes . . . *(Objectively:)* All the same, it sure is heavy.

SABINE

Wimp!

FEMALE PASSERBY *enters. She has a shawl on her head, a very garish, red and yellow shawl. Three quarters of the way across, she stops and says:*

Your fortune will have to wait until tomorrow. Anyway . . . I'm only passing by.

She leaves.

ÉTIENNE, *to Sabine.*

Do you love me?

SABINE

As if this was any place to ask a question like that! Right in this draft!

ÉTIENNE, *in a very calm voice.*

Even so, you can answer me. Do you love me?

SABINE

Well? And the suitcase? Haven't you rested enough yet?

ÉTIENNE, *calmer and calmer.*

Do you love me?

SABINE

I should have taken a second suitcase.

ÉTIENNE

I wonder if you love me.

SABINE

I was stupid to listen to you. We should have also taken the small suitcase, you know, the pigskin one. There were a heap of things I couldn't get into this one that I'm going to need.

ÉTIENNE

Sometimes I get the feeling I'm only a shadow to you, a ghost.

SABINE, *laughing.*

Exactly! Ghosts don't have biceps!

ÉTIENNE

Deep down you don't love me.

SABINE

I do, I do. You're getting on my nerves. Come on, take your suitcase, and let's go.

ÉTIENNE, *lifts the suitcase and lets it fall again.*

It's heavy.

SABINE, *raising her arms to the sky and tapping her foot.*

Oh my god! Mother! What a husband you dumped on me!

FEMALE PASSERBY, *enters. Sumptuous. Fur coat. In a great hurry. To the male beggar.*

No time to open my handbag. I'll get you next time.

MALE BEGGAR, *with servility.*

But of course, princess, but of course!

FEMALE PASSERBY

What do you expect, I'm only passing by.

She leaves.

ÉTIENNE, *big sigh.*

SABINE

What's up? You not feeling well? That's all I'd need now to look completely ridiculous.

ÉTIENNE

I want you to listen to me. I've something serious to tell you.

SABINE

Here?

ÉTIENNE

Here.

SABINE

Here? With the suitcase, the beggar, and the draft?

ÉTIENNE

Yes.

SABINE, *sits down on the suitcase.*

I'm listening.

ÉTIENNE

You don't love me.

SABINE

Are you saying that to make me cry or to make me laugh?

ÉTIENNE

I can see very well that you don't love me.

SABINE

What a moron! As if you weren't seeing only what I wanted you to see!

ÉTIENNE

Maybe. I feel like I'm worth less in your eyes than a pair of nail clippers, a run in a stocking, a shoe heel, a fashion designer's address, an elevator breakdown . . .

The female passerby crosses the stage, wandering aimlessly and humming an old melody.

ÉTIENNE, *in a distant voice.*

Around you, I feel like I'm becoming some sort of mist, a kind of gray smoke that barely rises, carried away by the wind, a kind of nothing.

SABINE

You're beginning to exasperate me. If you don't want to carry this suitcase anymore, I'll do it myself. *(She lifts the suitcase with difficulty, takes a couple of steps.)* I'll do it. *(She has to put it on the ground, near the male beggar. She sits down on it.)*

MALE BEGGAR

Madame, if you think that I'm going to offer to lug this heavy baggage around for even a considerable sum of money, then you're quite mistaken! *(With pride.)* I am a beggar, madame, I don't work!

SABINE

I'm not talking to you.

ÉTIENNE, *still in a distant voice.*

I'm dying of cold next to her, I'm so poorly loved . . . our life together . . . is that love?

SABINE, *to the male beggar.*

Seriously, will you listen to him?

MALE BEGGAR

Perhaps he's not well?

ÉTIENNE

. . . love . . . love . . .

SABINE

He sure can be stupid when he wants to.

MALE BEGGAR

And he often wants to?

ÉTIENNE

Any other woman . . .

SABINE

I'd like to see that.

MALE BEGGAR

Jealous?

ÉTIENNE

Any other woman.

SABINE

Don't make me laugh.

Enter the female passerby, head bare, hair in the wind.

ÉTIENNE

Mademoiselle!

She keeps walking.

ÉTIENNE

Mademoiselle . . .

She stops and turns.

ÉTIENNE

Mademoiselle . . .

FEMALE PASSERBY

Monsieur?

ÉTIENNE

Mademoiselle . . . uh . . . could you tell me . . . what the weather's like?

FEMALE PASSERBY

That has to be the first time someone's accosted me in that manner.

ÉTIENNE

Mademoiselle, please, don't misjudge me, I would really like to know: what's the weather like?

FEMALE PASSERBY

Simple enough question to answer. *(She opens her bag and takes out a round and flat object, a little bigger than a watch. She consults it.)* 776 millimeters. Set fair.

MALE BEGGAR, *imitating the sound of the wind.*

Woooooooooh . . . woooooooooooooh . . .

ÉTIENNE

You hear that?

FEMALE PASSERBY

Yet the hand is right on set fair.

MALE BEGGAR

Woooooooooh . . . woooooooooooh . . .

ÉTIENNE

The wind's howling.

FEMALE PASSERBY

Maybe this device is broken.

MALE BEGGAR

Woooooooooh . . . woooooooooooh . . .

ÉTIENNE, *raising his head.*

The clouds are racing along the surface of the sky like grey-hounds.

MALE BEGGAR

Woooooooooooh . . .

FEMALE PASSERBY

I'm sorry. It's broken.

ÉTIENNE

Too bad.

FEMALE PASSERBY

You could ask these people.

ÉTIENNE

That beggar?

MALE BEGGAR

Be polite, eh.

FEMALE PASSERBY

That lady?

ÉTIENNE

No point.

FEMALE PASSERBY

She wouldn't know?

SABINE

No.

FEMALE PASSERBY

I'm terribly sorry . . . Since I am unable to provide a satisfactory response to the question you have asked me, monsieur, I appeal to your gallantry for permission to withdraw. *(She curtseys.)*

ÉTIENNE, *bowing.*

Mademoiselle . . .

The female passerby makes a show of moving away.

ÉTIENNE, *calling her back.*

Mademoiselle . . .

FEMALE PASSERBY, *returning immediately.*

Monsieur?

ÉTIENNE

That device?

FEMALE PASSERBY

Yes?

ÉTIENNE

It's a barometer?

FEMALE PASSERBY

Precisely.

ÉTIENNE

So then . . . it tells what the weather will be like, not what it is now.

FEMALE PASSERBY

Are you sure?

ÉTIENNE

That's what they taught me at school.

FEMALE PASSERBY

But they also taught you that you can't know the future . . .

ÉTIENNE

Yes. Which to believe?

FEMALE PASSERBY, *gesture of despair.*

I don't know anymore.

ÉTIENNE, *stubbornly.*

If your barometer forecasts fair weather to come, maybe it's not broken?

FEMALE PASSERBY, *she takes the device out of her bag.*

It's now at 748 millimeters. Rain.

ÉTIENNE, *triumphant.*

And you can see that it isn't raining! Right now the weather's beautiful!

FEMALE PASSERBY

But soon . . . it's going to rain . . .

ÉTIENNE

Let's not think about it.

SABINE

That's just like him.

ÉTIENNE, *lively.*

This object's very elegant.

FEMALE PASSERBY

Really?

ÉTIENNE

Yes. It's completely flat. I wonder how it manages to work.

FEMALE PASSERBY

Oh! it's very sophisticated, there's very little mechanism inside.

ÉTIENNE

A present?

FEMALE PASSERBY

Yes.

ÉTIENNE

Uh . . . from a gentleman?

FEMALE PASSERBY

Yes.

ÉTIENNE

A gentleman . . . taller than me?

FEMALE PASSERBY

Oh yes.

ÉTIENNE

More . . . stylish?

FEMALE PASSERBY

Ohh yes.

ÉTIENNE

More . . . handsome? younger? richer?

FEMALE PASSERBY

Ohhhh yes.

ÉTIENNE

Ah!

MALE BEGGAR

Even so, if I was in his place, I wouldn't lose all hope.

SABINE

That's it! Give him advice!

FEMALE PASSERBY

Monsieur . . . you know . . . it's been two years and five months since I've seen him.

ÉTIENNE

You still love him?

FEMALE PASSERBY, *very conventional.*

The numbers are very nicely drawn, aren't they?

ÉTIENNE

Yes, and the letters too.

FEMALE PASSERBY

Storm . . . Variable . . . Set fair . . . If it were always set, it would never move, and it changes all the time . . . the weather.

ÉTIENNE

That makes you sad?

FEMALE PASSERBY

A little.

ÉTIENNE

Me too.

SABINE

Not me.

MALE BEGGAR

I couldn't give a rat's ass.

FEMALE PASSERBY, *again very conventional.*

A barometer's very useful, you know.

ÉTIENNE

Yes. *(Like a schoolboy who is reciting a lesson.)* As we said just now, it is used to forecast the weather.

FEMALE PASSERBY

Which isn't easy.

ÉTIENNE

This whole mishmash of cumulus, anticyclones, and isobars, what a mess! You go figure it out!

FEMALE PASSERBY

The snow, the sunburns, the rainbows, fogs, what fickleness!

ÉTIENNE

And we're still overlooking the thermometric aspect of the question.

FEMALE PASSERBY

You're interested in meteorology, monsieur?

ÉTIENNE

A little. I own an umbrella.

FEMALE PASSERBY

I've heard that there are little barometer houses from which a little guy with an umbrella comes out if it's going to rain and a little guy in shorts if it's going to be sunny.

MALE BEGGAR

I've seen some like that at the flea market.

SABINE

Will you take me there?

ÉTIENNE, *to the female passerby.*

We'll go together, if you like. You can find beautiful things there.

FEMALE PASSERBY

And such strange things. One time I found a little piece of something there. Yes. A little piece of something. That was it. *(Dreamy.)* Remarkable, isn't it? *(Abruptly.)* But . . . you did say just now, "we'll go together"?

ÉTIENNE

Yes, a second ago I said "we'll go together."

MALE BEGGAR

Tonight's too late.

SABINE

Thank goodness.

FEMALE PASSERBY

So, we should arrange to meet?

ÉTIENNE

I didn't dare . . .

FEMALE PASSERBY

But do . . .

ÉTIENNE

People generally go there on Sundays.

FEMALE PASSERBY

But the weather has to be nice.

ÉTIENNE

And what will the weather be like?

MALE BEGGAR

Lousy!

SABINE

Dreadful!

FEMALE PASSERBY

Lovely!

ÉTIENNE

Glorious!

MALE BEGGAR

If they don't agree with me, all they have to do is consult their barometer.

SABINE

They're not thinking.

ÉTIENNE, *looking afar.*

No clouds on the horizon, we've reason to hope.

FEMALE PASSERBY

I feel confident.

ÉTIENNE

I wish I suffered from rheumatism, then I could forecast the weather.

FEMALE PASSERBY

The dogs too, eating their grass.

ÉTIENNE

The rooster crowing to bed.

FEMALE PASSERBY

The birds flying low.

ÉTIENNE

The turned-over leaves of trees.

FEMALE PASSERBY

The spiders coming down from their webs.

ÉTIENNE

The closed dandelion blossoms.

FEMALE PASSERBY

You like the country, monsieur? Flowers, animals, nature?

ÉTIENNE, *fervently.*

Yes.

SABINE

The dirty liar.

FEMALE PASSERBY

We're going to get along so well.

ÉTIENNE

Yes . . . I love animals . . . big ones and little ones . . . trees . . . the hundred-year-old-ones and the shrubs . . . stones . . . rocks and pebbles . . .

FEMALE PASSERBY

I love big storms along the sea . . . the intense brightness of the sun at the top of mountains . . .

ÉTIENNE, *interrupting her.*

You did just say "we're going to get along so well"?

FEMALE PASSERBY

Yes. I just said "we're going to get along so well."

ÉTIENNE, *dreamily.*

We . . .

FEMALE PASSERBY

Yes. We . . .

SABINE, *shrugging her shoulders.*

Them!

ÉTIENNE

Yes. We.

FEMALE PASSERBY

Let's go.

ÉTIENNE

Let's go together.

MALE BEGGAR

They sound like they've made their minds up.

SABINE

That I'd like to see.

FEMALE PASSERBY

We'll go out into the street and we'll be in the night.

ÉTIENNE

But there'll be the moon, the stars . . . stars bigger than usual . . . shining brighter than usual . . .

FEMALE PASSERBY

We'll walk straight ahead.

ÉTIENNE

We'll cross the silent outskirts, heavy with their labor, and before daybreak we'll come to the edge of an immense forest.

FEMALE PASSERBY

Enormous black trees, where birds nest, birds that no one has ever seen.

ÉTIENNE

We'll enter this forest. Sometimes we'll encounter a herd of wild boars chased by hunters disappearing behind clusters of tall trees, whom we'll never see again . . . sometimes woodcutters at work, people who haven't read the newspaper for years . . .

FEMALE PASSERBY

. . . and sometimes, in vast clearings, a shepherd is watching over his flock. He knows what the weather will be! And he takes care of injuries by pronouncing words . . .

ÉTIENNE

. . . and sometimes benevolent, ruddy and timid dwarves, who run away at our approach.

FEMALE PASSERBY

We'll always return to the undergrowth where the dolmens and the covered paths sleep.[3]

ÉTIENNE

We'll have to cross torrents on stones thrown into the current.

FEMALE PASSERBY

And we'll come back up the other side of the valley, through the brushwood and the thickets.

ÉTIENNE

We'll walk for days and days, sometimes singing . . .

FEMALE PASSERBY

And often silent.

ÉTIENNE

One day, at dusk, we'll step onto a path strewn with fine sand, untouched by any feet.

FEMALE PASSERBY

And here shall appear . . .

ÉTIENNE

A castle.

FEMALE PASSERBY

All white and crenellated.

ÉTIENNE

The drawbridge will come down by itself.

FEMALE PASSERBY

We'll enter.

ÉTIENNE

The entire Universe will be summed up, our two existences developed, in its numberless rooms.

FEMALE PASSERBY

This corridor is the path of the Sun measured by the centipedes of its rays, the paths of our two lives at last joined together.

ÉTIENNE

This antechamber is the great frozen plowshare of the world, the plain and the desert, the common base of our associated desires.

FEMALE PASSERBY

This lounge is the repose of beings, the calm of things, the night of spaces, the peace of our union.

ÉTIENNE

This kitchen is the endless frothing of the Oceans, the absorption of planets, the deglutition of nebulas, the red lava of our passions.

FEMALE PASSERBY

This window looks onto the unity of crystals, that one onto the hazards of our destiny.

ÉTIENNE

This door is the dawn, that one is the corona.

FEMALE PASSERBY

We'll be alone and masters amidst the crowd of atoms, and the labyrinth's perfect mazes shall never separate us.

ÉTIENNE

The world as our subject shall never be able to rise up against the excellence of our ties.

FEMALE PASSERBY

We'll persist in our double being through every transformation, every becoming.

ÉTIENNE

You'll be my inextinguishable lamp, my beautiful worry, my enchanted palace.

FEMALE PASSERBY

You'll be my thousand and second night, my breaking day, my nighttime visitor.

ÉTIENNE

We'll exist together.

FEMALE PASSERBY

We exist together.

ÉTIENNE, *taking her into his arms.*

I love you.

FEMALE PASSERBY

I love you.

At this moment a violent ringing of bell.

MALE BEGGAR

Ah! they're closing down.

SABINE, *waking up.*

I do believe I was asleep.

MALE BEGGAR

It's the sweep.

SABINE

The sweep?

MALE BEGGAR

The last metro, you stupid little goose.

He leaves. New ringing of bell. Étienne and the female passerby are looking into each other's eyes. They don't move in the slightest. Sabine gets up.

SABINE, *curtly.*

Étienne!

Étienne doesn't move.

SABINE

Étienne!

Étienne doesn't move.
New ringing of bell.

SABINE

Étienne, you hear me? The last metro!

At these words, he jumps.

ÉTIENNE

What?

SABINE

I said it's the last metro.

ÉTIENNE

Ah! *(To the female passerby:)* Mademoiselle . . . mademoiselle . . . I'm sorry . . . you understand . . . *(He takes some steps backward.)* . . . the last metro. *(He takes the suitcase and leaves with Sabine.) (Turning back with a gesture of regret.)* . . . the last metro.

FEMALE PASSERBY, *with an equally regretful gesture.*

What do you expect . . . I was only passing by.

They each go their separate way.

CURTAIN

The crossing had been most unpleasant, and, reaching Boulogne, Alice had not yet recovered from the difficult events that had adorned her trip. She therefore did not really notice what was happening around her when she set foot on French soil. She left her suitcase in the hands of a customs officer with a big mustache and for the time being felt unconcerned about its fate—even though she had taken so much trouble packing it, using the method her French book had advised, which consisted of noting on a sheet of paper the different objects that have to do with the hair and that you should take with you, then those that have to do with the forehead, then with the eyebrows, the eyelids, etc. All the way down to those that concern the soles of the shoes beginning with the heel *first*; then, of course, you lose the sheet of paper that you had taken so much trouble drawing up. But *Alice* hadn't lost *her* sheet of paper and she was sure—and very proud—that she had left out *nothing* from her suitcase. And there she was letting it go, without a worry in the world. She was no more worried about the fate of her older sister, for that matter, who had vanished into the mob that was pushing up against the customs house, while the locomotive could be heard puffing strenuously while waiting to take the travelers to the capital; and Alice was surprised that it was puffing in this manner since it was at rest, whereas *men* only puff when they've been running. But, after all, men are *men,* whereas locomotives are machines, and they probably don't always know how they should behave.

"Not at all," said a man completely covered in plaster and flour.

Alice raised her eyes to look at the individual who was contradicting her so rudely; she assumed it was a worker, and she wasn't surprised, for she had been taught that workers, especially French workers, don't have good manners. She thus forgave him to herself, but she was quite determined not to continue the conversation; she had moreover also been taught that one shouldn't talk to people who have less than a thousand pounds income, unless it's to give them orders.

"It might have run to get here," continued the individual. And he began to look at Alice with wide eyes, as if he were waiting for a reply.

"Locomotives don't run," replied Alice.

She reproached herself for having so quickly forgotten her good intentions, but after all there was no one there to see her, and no one would know, *in England*, that she had spoken to a French worker. And then, after all, maybe he wasn't a worker.

"That one runs," said the white man. "It ran to come here and get you."

"Even if it ran," said Alice, "it didn't come to get me in particular."

"You're wrong, mademoiselle."

Ah, thought Alice, he said: "mademoiselle." He's more polite than I thought, although he's always contradicting me rather crudely. Perhaps he has two thousand pounds income.

"I came specially to look for you, with my locomotive. You'll get onto the tender with me."

Alice was thrilled to be making the trip on the tender rather than in those ugly, black cars, which she had seen from the bridge. And, forgetting the suitcase altogether, she followed the white man.

On the platform there was a tremendous hustle and bustle. People were squeezing themselves into the cars and were scuttling about the train like ants about a dead caterpillar. For that matter, *they were* ants.

"What about *them*?" asked Alice.

"They think they're going to leave, but they never leave. The locomotive isn't hooked onto their train."

"They have no idea?"

"That doesn't matter to them since they have their ticket."

The white man shrugged his shoulders.

Reaching the locomotive, which was whitewashed, Alice . . .

.   .   .   .

(They get on.)

The white man put a few shovelfuls of flour into the boiler, pulled on a piece of string and the locomotive got moving.

On the platform the ants continued to squeeze into the cars, not worrying about the locomotive's departure.

There was a lot of flour in the tender.

"In England," said Alice proudly, "our locomotives run on coal."

"Here, they run on flour," replied the white man calmly, sitting down with a tired and dreamy air before a little whitewood table. He looked at his watch, sighed, and lit a little candle that he fastened onto the table by making the tallow run.

"In *all* countries," said Alice firmly, "locomotives run on coal."

"Not in France," he replied.

"And why is that?"

"Not everyone can eat white bread."

Alice reflected a moment; and, as she was now used to peculiar thoughts and that she indeed thought that in France people were even more peculiar than elsewhere, she said:

"So, who eats coal?"

"Miners, of course," replied the white man. "Here, everyone eats the product of their labor: masons eat bricks, steelworkers nails, writers books."

"In England too," said Alice who wanted to be amiable, "they're called bookworms."

"You're wrong," said the white man absentmindedly but with utmost rigor.

He's becoming crude again, thought Alice, and there he is claiming to know English better than me.

"A bookworm," said the other, "is a gentleman who reads a lot of books, but who doesn't write them. Whereas with us an author has the right to eat only his own books, and other people don't have the right to eat them."

In her heart, Alice felt pity for the poor writers, for she didn't think that books were a very pleasant food; she herself had sometimes tried to chew notebook paper, but she never managed to digest it.

"On what kind of paper are books printed?" she inquired.

"On rice paper, of course," replied the white man, placidly.

At this moment, Alice heard a bang and a bullet whistled, passing before her nose. She was very afraid, but naturally didn't want to let it show. As the white man made no comment, she asked, timidly:

"What's that?"

"What?"

"The noise we just heard," said Alice.

A second bullet whistled.

"That," said Alice.

"That? It's a level-crossing keeper."

"In England," said Alice, "the level-crossing keepers don't shoot at the trains."

"It's an old habit of theirs," replied the white man who seemed not to be surprised or scandalized by anything. "They're all retired hoteliers."

Alice didn't really see the connection, for she didn't think that hoteliers hunted, but, since the completely white man was saying so, she could only believe him.

"When they're working," he added "they lay in tooth and nail."

Alice shuddered, and without understanding, was very pleased all the same about the beneficial effects of retirement.

Meanwhile the train was running at a good speed. From time to time, the white man put a shovelful of flour into the boiler, but he especially kept an eye on his candle, which for that matter didn't seem to reduce or melt even though its brightness didn't dim in the slightest. Alice, tired from the trip, dozed off on the heap of flour. When she awoke, it was night. The candle was still burning. The white man seemed to have been waiting for her to wake up, because he appeared joyous when she did. He immediately held out a quill to her.

"What must I do?" asked Alice.

"Well! But I'm lending you my quill."

"Why?"

"To write a word."

"But *what* word?" asked Alice.

The white man stood gaping. Alice remained quill in hand. What was more, she noticed that there was no ink.

"That's not important," said the white man. "Write without ink."

He looked with despair at the candle, which, suddenly, began to diminish in intensity.

"Just one word!" he exclaimed.

"I'll try to please him," said Alice to herself and, handling the quill with decision, she wrote, in French, *The Moon*:

"La Lune."

"That's two words," Pierrot said sternly. "I only asked you to write one."

Alice decided to be pleasant to him, hesitated between crossing out the first or the second. She opted for the first. There thus remained:

"   Lune."

"There's a spelling error," observed Pierrot.

"I don't think so," said Alice timidly.

"Lunne takes two n's."

"I couldn't know French better than him," Alice said to herself. She asked: "Why?"

"Because there are two," replied Pierrot. "The full one and the new one."

Alice thought: "what a funny astronomy," but she didn't want to annoy him. So she added an n. That made:

"   Lunne."

Pierrot still didn't seem satisfied.

"It's not very round."

"If other n's were added?" suggested Alice.

And that gave:

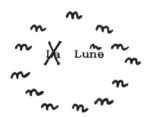

I eventually came up along the sea, on a boulevard. There were twenty or so boats in harbor, with their lights, which were dancing, crowned with real Le Havre weather: rain, wind, storm, a good half of the barometer dispersed into the atmosphere. When I left this city, more than twenty-five years ago, I had come, all alone, like a man, to gaze one last time at the sea.[1] That day, like today, it was raining, windy, storming. And I found all that to be very poetic; it's amazing that I didn't write a poem on the spot, probably because I wasn't able to; in those days, I believed I was going to become a poet in Paris, but that didn't happen until a good many years later (or so I believe). At that time, I dare say that in walking along the sea that way, in the rain, I was thinking that the poem was going to come; it's what we call the purity of adolescence, the time when one is full of contempt for literature. Now, after years of literature (practiced in a public manner) it's not to seek a subject for a poem or a short story or even a novel that I was going for a stroll on this rainy November day. I'm writing about it now, why not, but that wasn't really my intention. As if it was necessary that I write about everything. I grind my teeth when people think that I do this or that or that I go to see this or that, so I can then produce some passage of a novel. What a layman's notion. As if one couldn't live like anyone else. What an absurdity. That day, then, a few days ago, I was on this boulevard, at night, along the sea on which it was raining as much as it was upon the land ('nother absurdity, right? What a mess, what a loss of strength; when the dams need it) simply because I was fed up with Paris and that I was working off one hell of a fit of despair there, without wanting for all that to leave for

Cameroon or Mauritania so as to disguise my blues as a solid colonial depression. A friend was going to Le Havre by car, I got into the car and the whole, effectively, arrived at Le Havre. Then he went his way, I went mine. Fuck no, when I think about it, it's not the desire to transform this gloomy situation into writing that brought me to the boulevard along the sea. I've never wanted to transform anything at all into writing, when there's anything to transform in the first place.

Le Havre was a dreary enough city between the wars. It's a port, of course. There were brothels, bistros (one of which had a mechanical violin, a peculiar instrument manufactured in Hamburg), sailors who threw punches, sirens, ship owners and cafe owners. They shot cinema films there, which were shot badly. And then it rains, as a general rule. It was rather funny during the other war. People (military in general) had come from all parts of the world (in question), everyone was swarming about (after all that, twenty years later, I took some liberty with the truth, my apologies).[2] The other one didn't go too badly, even better than the one in '70. But during this war, it took one hell of a blow. Le Havre was one of the most bombed cities, the most, even, quantitatively, after Berlin and one other (I think I read that in *Le Monde*, the well-informed paper). In two days, flames and bedlam leveled the center of the city to the ground, and the dead, they didn't even get counted. They're still some there beneath the stones and the scrap iron that were put into piles, piles, moreover, that aren't very large or very high. Last year, in September, one year later, it was not very packed down yet, and there was also a lot of dust. With the rain, the dust settles, like the rest. It's all what one would call razed, as if from the Pont Royal (a Parisian bridge I've chosen at random) one could see the Gare Montparnasse (with nothing in between, nothing higher than a few centimeters, and the piles in question, not very high, nor very large, as I said). That's the center; the outskirts remain, the suburbs, that's where Le Havre's life is, in places that in my day were miles from anywhere and that have since become centers, the Rond-Point, for example; in '14, the groceries that were selling Kub bouillon there were ransacked and in '17, the wogs were defenestrated.

After leaving Salacrou,[3] I arrived in that area around five-thirty, six o'clock. I passed in front of a post office that, in my childhood, seemed to me to be on the borders of the real world. It was still there. I sought, I found and I sent a postcard showing the ruins (I found that to be very symbolic). There were quite a lot of people in the streets, it was "lively." (But almost no more Americans. Last year, on this spot, two small vans would take the girls to the *dansigne*, at a camp near Harfleur. On one of the vans, "there'll be lots to eat" had been written in chalk.) It began to rain. I passed in front of the Communist Party office (they were selling a brochure there on the reconstruction of Le Havre, the great French port). It rained more and more. I went into a little bar, on a little street perpendicular to one that had been called, before the other war, the Cours de la République, and which is perhaps still called so today. Inside was a rather ghastly whore and three or four guys who were trafficking pea coats, English cigarettes, and women's shoes. It never occurs to me to traffic, perhaps I could have gotten a good deal. The traffickers eventually left, so I followed suit, which didn't keep the rain from falling. I followed a boulevard that changed names several times, owing to the wars, I imagine; between that of '70 and that of '14, it was called Strasbourg. The left side, when leaving the station, looks like it's in pieces; the other side consists of a small number of ruins and, what's more, a German blockhouse transformed into an American bar. Down the stairs and you're there. I was the only customer. It was freezing, and then a blockhouse, even disused, is not exactly amusing. It may be bearable to be completely alone in a cafe, but in a posh spot like that, it can be frightening. I didn't stay long; the *martinese*, moreover, weren't exactly first-rate; the barmen were quite willing to direct me to a place where I could go have something to eat. There was my hotel on top of the hill, but it was far, so they recommended the X to me. I had trouble finding it. It's in a neighborhood I hardly ever went in as a kid (although—funny "although"—I was

84

born around there), and now after this shock, it is as if Le Havre's inhabitants no longer know where their streets are. Even so, I managed to discover it, after a good deal of meandering about in the rain.

It was a very small restaurant with five or six tables and what one would call a modest appearance. I ate very well there, and not too expensively: some serious black market. At one table, there were three young men who were trafficking all sorts of things between them; they were good-looking and of the unemployed members-of-the-Resistance type. At another, there were two rather drunk hookers in the company of two not very young Americans in civvies, one with glasses. They were eating nothing but oysters, the girls were having a good laugh while jabbering all sorts of languages (there were traces of German). One of them was Kabyle; she began to speak Arabic with one of the guys from the other table, a Berber. Her friend got up to make a call. The phone was in the dining room. She asked for number 38 at Livarot. The Americans seemed to be getting fed up, wanting to move on to more serious things. They didn't like the young guys at the other table. One of the Americans got up and made as if to take off his jacket for a fight, but the tart who was returning from the telephone calmed him down, she shoved an oyster into his gullet, he kept quiet. Anyway, once again, they ate nothing but oysters. Meanwhile, I was making a pig of myself while drinking Traminer. Two new guys entered, one, hat pulled over his eyes, in a gabardine raincoat. The owner greeted him with a "hello, Jacqueline." His companion was very young. The telephone rang: it was Livarot calling back. The girl ran. It involved packages, parcels, packets. I almost asked her to include me, Livarot cheese is first-rate, but complicated stories of fresh supplies are tiresome.

When I go out, it's raining. There are large holes of water. I wander across the devastation. I nearly smash my face in a number of times. The mud climbs up my legs. My socks get damp. There's a heap of rather interesting scrap iron. A child (not yet in bed at that hour?) is rummaging about in it. Further off, a small group of huts: a butcher's shop; in the distance, a lit cinema. I lean, a little drunk, against a low wall reconstructed in no very defined way and I train my eye to take note of all that (not to write on this subject, that only came after, but to see how fucking awful the scenery is).

Little by little, I come alongside the sea. I'm finally there. There are twenty or so boats in harbor, with their lights that dance, crowned with real Le Havre weather. Last year, but it was in full daylight, the Americans demolished the German pillboxes that were there. There were heaps of (to me) extraordinary machines, one in particular with big jaws that gobbled up cement, shat pebbles and pissed sand. Now, thanks to these labors, there's a beach. Naturally, at this hour, in this weather, no one's there. All of that's fucking deserted. I splash about, climbing back up to Sainte-Adresse.

I see lights in the direction of the tollhouse. In front of it, a character dressed like a *groume* (whom I discover to be a woman) waylays two big British navy captains. They let themselves be tempted. I enter behind them. In the first room, there's a *pimpon* table. On the left, one passes on to the bar. In the back, a *dansigne*. There's an orchestra of three individuals who come very close to making a respectable noise. A host and hostess are pretending to *souigne* dance, they don't know how, but they ask the barman for black coffee. One of the captains dances with the *groumesse* who has taken off her greatcoat. A gentleman enters, in gabardine (again, but this one's covered with stains). Without taking off his oozing hat, he invites the washroom attendant, and there they are cutting a rug. Then some bourgeois arrive.

I drink two liqueur brandies. I'm bored stiff. I split. I try to find my hotel. It's tough. Luckily I meet a gas man who kindly shows me the way.

From the top of the hill, I look at the dejection. I think about my little ruins, my personal ruins. In the harbor everything's slogging away. (To import coffee?) Heaps of lights. Things are hopping. Or are pretending to hop. And then after, dark zones, ruins, sluttishness, stupidity. Paris is one hell of a disguise, a tiny bit antiquated. The real France is there. In front of my eyes. Getting rained on.

As for me, my apologies, I'm a poet. Ruins, sluttishness, stupidity, all that always gladdens a poet's heart.

A Muslim soldier asks me where he can find the Saint-Marie cemetery. What the fuck does he want to go there for at this hour?

In the end I find my hotel. There I sleep.

For a ghost, I again draw the reader's attention to Merdle.

Alain, *En lisant Dickens* (Reading Dickens), p. 41.

As far as I can remember, I've always been afraid of anything that might give me any trouble; I thus was successively afraid of the bogeyman, wax figures in the Dupuytren museums, places overly frequented by vehicles, hoodlums, flowerpots that fall on heads, ladders, the clap, the pox, the Gestapo, V-2s. Peace did not, of course, in any way ease these alarms; thus, the other evening, I'm eating some chestnut purée, and I begin to dream that I'm in a *djip* and that the driver wasn't going to avoid a thick pillar, I see it coming, I tell myself that we're crashing into it, there it is, we crashed into it, everything goes black; in the black-ness, I say to myself: I'm dead, I say to myself: so that's what it's like when you die, and then I wake up, my stomach distended and my heart beating. I turn the lights on, I look at my watch, it's two o'clock, two o'clock in the morning, still pretty early, and I get up to take a piss. As I don't use a chamberpot, I have to go to the toilet. There's a long corridor. I go down it saying: if this, if that. I manage to scare myself, and I go into the john quite happy to be able to close the door behind me, to make this long story short, and feel at home, and not only to close the door, but also to turn the lock.

I piss.

I pull the chain.

When the hygienic gurgling quieted down, I sensed the pres-ence of nothingnesses in the corridor, without any atmosphere of existence, which made me warm in the teeth, cold under the fingernails, general horripilation. An abject fright grabbed hold of my soul, and, putting my head in my hands, I sat down on the toilet seat, bemoaning my vile fate. The presence of these nothingnesses without any atmosphere of existence was obviously the fruit (immaculately conceived) of my imagination taken to the brinks of shittery under the influence of the chestnut purée. This explanation, valid from the point of view of many an ism, could not help, of course, but fully satisfy my penchant for philosophical studies, but did nothing, alas! to prevent the existence of the nothingnessing atmospheres of presence from lurking about in the corridor, thirsting after cerumen and depravity, swollen with their labile pointlessness and their inappropriate onanism.

An hour passed.

I felt the ambiences full of the nothingness of their present existence flatten themselves against the door of the bog, dribble their loathsome purulence against it and twist around the doorknob, like a lemon upon the cone that will extract its acidic and citric liquid. They deeply disgusted me. And as for myself, I remained seated on the toilet seat, bemoaning my fate, and I could see, blurring through my tears, the parallelepipedic shape and the downy touch of my sack, where I had dreamily smashed in my face in a *djîp*.

I would very much have liked to have gone back to it, to go to sleep, to try to, but there was the atmosphere of existences without presence and without nothingness that, lurking in the corridor, prevented me from giving the lock the 180° rotation that would have been the first step toward hitting the hay in which I was longing t'snorze. I'm timorous, certainly, as I said, I realize it, but I've never sought to avoid bitter reality, I've always looked it inna face. Since I was stuck for more than two hours in this spot that is sometimes described, and childishly so, as "little," I had to resign myself and found a society there of which I would be at once Robinson and Friday, and, just as the hero of the British novel saw trunks full of workman's treasures brought by a sea both benevolent and subject to a Neptune named Defoe, I thus discovered in a little cabinet the first elements of my Robinsonism in the form of a toolbox very decently stocked with nails, hammers, pliers, screws, and hooks, not to mention a folding rule that measured twelve decimeters, an archaeological trace of a duodecimal-based civilization.

But the presences without nothingness of ambient existence continued to lurk in the corridor, leaving their trail of preternatural, abulic, and subperceptible snail-slobber.

Five hours trickled along the toilet chain, which communicated, through some architectural subtlety, with the Empire clock next door.

The discovery of the toolbox restored my courage. I got up, I took a second piss, I pulled the foresaid chain and began to hammer nails into the wall, this attitude having at that moment, for me, no precise goal. I simply demonstrated in this manner my ambient presence of existing nothingness. And as I overheard, at my bedroom doorstep, having gotten up in the middle of the night from having eaten too much chestnut purée and desirous of having a piss, the muffled sound of the hammer being wielded in the toilet by a nothingness present in an existing ambiance, I made an about-turn, scared shitless, and went back to bed.

A man entered the cafe, which created some mist. He settled down at the bar, hauling himself onto a stool, which roused the appearance of a cafe owner with a white jacket and a fierce appearance. All the tables were taken and the people at them were minding their own business. The waiters were yawning. The newcomer took a good look around him, no, there wasn't a single free seat, so he replied to the question that his adversary had just asked him.

"I'll have a glass of water," he said.

"Very good, monsieur," replied the barman.

He examined this fellow with respect and got cracking. He took a large beer glass, swirled a piece of ice in it, threw the iceberg away with disgust, employed a carafe of water, set the misted-over glass down on the bar, placed it side by side with the receptacle.

"There you are, monsieur," said this man.

The other poured out a glass of water and drank a small amount of it. Then he kept still, dreaming. The people at the tables, men, women, were minding their own business. The barman had plunged into other labors. Outside it was cold. The hands of the clock, the wall clock—and electric into the bargain—sped metaphysically after each other. The rather chubby cashier was dozing.

The man took the glass in his hands and sampled another small amount of water. The band began playing a dance tune. Some people got up and, taking hold of each other, described intricate curves on the floor. The barman surreptitiously knocked back one hell of a drink of gin. A newsagent entered, then left, overwhelmed by the printed universe that he was carrying under his arm and by the rottenness of the world, real or transcribed. The hands had just caught up with each other on the clock face, something that happens twenty times a day. Finally, the door opened again and a woman entered.

She immediately spotted the man she was looking for and sat down next to him. The barman loomed up.

"Give me another glass of water," said the man, "this one got warm."

"You wouldn't like mineral water this time?"

"No," replied the man.

"And for mademoiselle?" asked the barman.

"Nothing," replied the woman.

"And will that be all for today?" asked the barman with very slight insolence.

"Yes," said the man, "that'll be all."

The barman served the new glass of water. He put a piece of ice in it.

"Well?" the woman asked the man.

"Well, nothing, what a life," murmured the man.

"It's no fun," said the woman.

She looked around her.

A guy in glasses was dancing with a prostitute, doing some fancy moves for the gallery and smiling at the piano player. He seemed a little drunk and not entirely at ease.

"An accountant who made off with the till," said the man.

"You think so?" said the woman.

"Yes, it's obvious."

Some guys were dancing with their hats on their heads.

"It's a fun place," said the man.

"Yes," said the woman.

The music stopped and the violin player swung his instrument at arm's length while chatting with a woman who was alone at a table. The dancers went back to their tables. The accountant did so with exhibitionism. A horse, who was at the bar, leaned over and asked if the woman would have a drink with him, as well as the gentleman who was accompanying her.

"What does he want?" said the man. "Is he asking you to dance?"

"No," murmured the woman, "I think he wants to offer us a drink."

The horse had gotten off of his stool and was bowing before them, making grand gestures with his forepaws. He was searching for words.

"You," he explained, "you, both of you, you have a drink with me."

The man looked at him with an annoyed air.

"No, thank you," he said coolly.

The horse didn't seem to be his natural self. The woman was a bit terrified. The man asked her how her aunt Charlotte was getting along. She was very important to them, Aunt Charlotte. But the presence of the horse made her uncomfortable to talk about her, about Aunt Charlotte. She shied away. The horse was patiently waiting for them to bring their little private conversation to an end.

Handsomely bribed by the accountant on a spree, the orchestra had started up again and dipped into a medley of 1900 waltzes. The horse waved his big legs and, taking advantage of a lapse in the conversation relative to Aunt Charlotte, uttered these words:

"You maybe think that I'm intoxicated? Certainly not. Certainly not. Certainly not."

He punctuated his words with graceful curvets. Then he looked at them, rolling terrible eyes. He was a big, completely black nag, a little rawboned, with very shiny hooves, and his tail in corkscrew curls and tied tight with a purple ribbon.

"No, no, I'm not drunk, but I don't always know how to weigh my gestures, my language, my words, my . . ."

He seemed to reflect:

"My conversations. I need to . . . I need to . . ."

He seemed to reflect:

"To adapt myself. Yes, that's it: to adapt myself."

He gave a large smile that revealed a broad yellowish set of teeth, in the interstices of which one could see, here and there, bits of hay.

"To adapt myself," he repeated complacently.

"He's sloshed," murmured the man.

"Do you have a cigarette?" the woman asked him without paying attention to the horse. "I forgot mine."

The man held out a pack of Gauloises. But the horse, swiftly thrusting a hoof into his saddlebags, rooted out a box adorned in red and gold. He opened it. It contained pieces of straw twisted and woven into the form of cigarillos. He offered one to the woman.

"They must be filthy," murmured the woman.

"Don't let him push you around," the man quietly advised her.

"No, thank you," said the woman, "I prefer Gauloises."

The horse turned to the man who declined.

"Me too. Anyway, I never smoke after nine in the evening."

The horse looked at them suspiciously. They gave him an amiable smile. The woman lit her Gauloise. The man lit nothing at all. The horse beat his flanks and racked his brains. Finally, he put the box back into his saddlebag. At this moment the accountant on a spree smashed his face on the floorboards and the waiters began to throw streamers in their pretense of having a really good time.

"You don't think," said the man, "that we could try to hit up Aunt Charlotte?"

"She's so stingy," said the woman.

"Even so, in our situation."

"You try," said the woman. "She likes you."

"Yeah, I know. What a drag. What a life."

The horse was solemnly waiting for them to finish. After this last interjection, he judged the moment right to intervene.

"I also have an aunt," he said shrewdly. "And you're going to have a drink with me," he added rather more menacingly.

"What a," began the man, but he interrupted himself with a mouthful of water.

"Are you Houyhnhnm?"[1] asked the woman politely.

This question seemed to delight the horse. He again started to wave his big legs and roll his eyes.

"Not Houyhnhnm," he neighed. "Not Houyhnhnm. Not Houyhnhnm at all. Guess?"

And he leaned over toward them, his eyes shining, as if they were a peck of oats. Or even two.

"Not Houyhnhnm," he insisted. "Guess."

Faced with this mystery, the man and the woman didn't know how to reply.

"When could we go see her?" the man asked the woman.

"No, no," the horse cried out with a pleasant smile. "Not talk other thing. Guess."

"Houyhnhnm," said the man resignedly.

"No, no, not Houyhnhnm, not Houyhnhnm."

"Then we don't know," said the man resignedly.

The horse's smile became more and more paternal.

"Come on. Try harder. A famous city. Guess. Guess."

"He's a pain in the ass," said the man between his teeth.

But the horse still had a pleasant smile on and was still showing his own, his teeth.

The woman made another attempt:

"Auteuil?"

"No," exclaimed the horse, absolutely thrilled by this little game.

"Le Tremblay?"

"No, no."

"Chantilly?"

"No, no, no."

She listed other racecourses. But it was always no.

Finally the man said to the horse, finishing his glass of water:

"We don't know."

And to the woman:

"You're not thirsty? Don't you want a glass of water?"

"*I'm* buying you a drink," declared the horse with authority. "Let's leave that aside for now. So you not know? I mean, you don't know?"

"No," said the woman.

"Well, I'm from Troyes."

"Ah," went the others.

"I'm Trojan," insisted the nag.

"Ah, Trojan," said the others.

"Yup, I'm from Troyes," neighed the horse, at the height of excitement.

"He's not drunk," said the man, "he's drugged."

"Anyway," said the horse from Troyes, "I'm going to show you my pedigree."

He thrust back one of his forepaws and rummaged about in his saddlebags. He pulled out a filthy notebook, which he began to leaf through feverishly. Some pages seemed to be stained with manure.

"You see, eh, I was born in Troyes. But papa was born in Saratoga and mama at Epsom. They had two legs both of them. Me mean: two legs each. But I've ancestors who had four."

"No?" went the man with a dubious air.

He turned to the barman and ordered two glasses of water.

"Tomorrow you're going to be broke again," said the woman.

"And will that be all for today?" asked the barman.

"Yes," said the man.

"Stop, stop," said the horse to the barman. "I'm buying a drink."

The barman hesitated.

"Give us a glass of water for two anyhow," said the man.

"Yes, yes," said the horse, "in a little while we're going to have a drink together, but still me a thing to make you guess. I mean: I still have a question to ask you."

"Go on," said the man with a half-hearted and sour look that spread from the corner of his mouth over his entire face.

The horse put his pedigree back into his saddlebags and took out his smokable hay.

"No? You don't smoke?"

"No," said the man and the woman in chorus.

He slipped a cigarillo between two teeth and held it out to the barman's lighter. He took a few puffs, which he sent to the ceiling. His face had mellowed, his eyes seemed to betray a certain satisfaction. And even pretension. He spoke again in these terms:

"You'll obviously never guess my occupation."

"You're in sports!" suggested the woman timidly.

"I play a little from time to time," replied the horse placidly. "Indeed, I run now and then, but only in gentlemen's races. No, that's not it. I'm a student."

"In botany?" asked the man, trying to make an effort at irrationality.

"Not bad, not bad," replied the horse with an important air. "No, in genetics."

"In what?" asked the woman.

Suddenly interested, the barman tried to join the conversation.

"Monsieur," he said to the horse, "is interested in genetics?"

"Precisely."

There was a short interlude. The musicians put away some refreshments. The accountant on a spree had conclusively collapsed into the arms of a loose woman. Only a little hubbub conveyed the intellectual life of the people present.

A sort of bored respect surrounded the horse. He was quite satisfied by it. He began to hold forth:

"Yes," he said, "it's a science that concerns my family in particular. Just imagine."

He surveyed the vicinity with his large eyes to see if everyone was paying attention.

"Just imagine," he continued, "grandpa was a centaur and grandma a mare. So, according to the laws of Mendel, here's the result."

And he patted his chest with little, somewhat pedantic, hoof taps.

"But," he added with pride, "I've a sister who has two legs. She's a dancer at Tabarin."

He smiled shrewdly.

"You can see her in one scene in particular: The Fight of the Amazons."

He took his time as he sent a puff of hay smoke toward the ceiling.

"She plays the role of a little horse."

Another pause.

"These are the little ironies of life," he concluded.

The barman burst out laughing, enchanted.

The man and the woman tried to grimace.

"He's sure keeping us waiting," grumbled the man under his breath.

The barman's sharp ear caught hold of the allusion. He asked cheerfully:

"So, what'll it be for everyone?"

"That's right, that's right," neighed the horse, again making uncoordinated gestures with his forepaws. "A drink, I'm buying you a drink."

"What would you like?" the man asked the woman.

The woman hesitated a bit.

"A gin fizz," she said eventually.

"A gin fizz for mademoiselle," confirmed the barman with growing enthusiasm.

"I'll have a gin fizz as well," said the man.

"And for monsieur?" the barman asked the horse.

"Gin fizz," said the horse.

"Three gin fizzes it is," bellowed the barman.

He hurled himself onto his appliances, while the band launched another attack on a new selection of 1900 tunes, by general demand of the dancers in fedoras.

"You're right," the woman said to the man, "there's nothing else to do. You're gonna have to hit up Aunt Charlotte."

"I'll go tomorrow," said the man. "But it's no fun."

"And how old do you think I am?" the horse asked them.

They turned their heads to him.

"Forty," said the woman in a dull voice.

"You're crazy," the man said to her in a low voice. "A horse has croaked at that age."

He turned to the horse:

"No," he said. "Two and a half, three."

"Right," said the horse with satisfaction.

Then his face suddenly changed expression and became completely cold.

"But," he asked the man, "why you say: croak?"

"Me?" replied the man with a feigned air of innocence.

"Yes, you," said the horse. "Why you say: croak?"

"Ah yes," went the man with a casual air. "Croak. Croak."

"Yes, croak," said the horse.

He began to make big gestures with his forepaws, then abruptly delivered a vigorous kick into the void. The dancers moved away respectfully.

"Croak," he neighed, "you said croak."

"I was talking about Aunt Charlotte," said the man.

"But yes, that's it," exclaimed the woman. "We were just now talking about Aunt Charlotte."

"Who is soon going to croak," added the man.

They began to laugh knowingly.

The horse had apparently calmed down. He looked at them now with a stern, oval eye.

"Here they are, three gin fizzes for everyone," said the barman, setting the glasses down before the customers.

"No," went the horse.

With a deft but dignified movement of his hoof, he slid the two other gin fizzes in front of his.

"The three for me," he said to the barman.

He turned to his two friends with a calm and majestic air.

"Aunt Charlotte," the man explained to him, "she's going to croak soon."

The horse didn't reply.

"What a pain in the ass," said the man to the woman. "Come on."

They got off of their stools.

"Good night," the barman said to them impartially.

"Good night," they replied.

They stopped on the doorstep.

It had started to snow.

"You're going to get your feet wet," said the man.

"What do you expect," said the woman.

They turned and saw the horse, who had already downed two gin fizzes. The horse pretended to not see them. He began to drink the third. With a straw.

They left.

"Awful weather," said the man.

"Don't worry," said the woman.

"Tomorrow I'll hit up Aunt Charlotte," said the man.

Stockbreeders take great care with the tails of their animals. A cousin of mine, for example, fastened little lead disks to his German shepherd's tail so that it wouldn't take on the curve of a hunting horn. He got caudal abscesses, the dog. Everyone will also agree that there's something barbaric about nicking a horse's tail. What the hell, if the unlucky nag isn't thoroughbred, don't torture him so he can look like a dandy. That's precisely what one of them was saying to me the other day, in a bar next to the statue of Serpollet.

"Of course," he was telling me, "my owner only managed to make me a cocktail, not an Arabian."

As he only looked at most like a Percheron to me, I didn't really know how to console him.

The barman came forward to ask the animal:

"You're a cocktail . . . you?"

"You could address me as monsieur . . . you!" replied the quadruped.

"Quiet down," I said to the barman. "There are lots of words in English that we Parisians don't know. It's a very rich language."

"All the same, monsieur doesn't expect me to believe that he's a cocktail!" exclaimed the man of the trade.

"This waiter's starting to get on my nerves," muttered the horse. "He's asking for a hoof in the teeth."

"One would have to consult an English-French dictionary," I suggested.

"A cocktail!" murmured the barman contemptuously.

The horse said nothing but the skin along his flanks was rippling with brief and menacing undulations.

I tried to work things out:

"Do you remember," I began, "do you remember this story, a rather amusing one, someone enters a bar, he asks for something to drink, he makes a slight error in his order and there's something extraordinary about *him* too, but it's in the order that all the story's wit lies, I can't quite remember the details anymore, what was so extraordinary about this customer . . ."

"He was a horse," said the barman.

"And the drink was a coquetèle," added the horse who had regained all his cool.

He pronounced this word, hammering out each syllable.

"A coquetèle," he insisted.

Then he neighed.

So I put a banknote down on the bar and I left. I wasn't about to linger around that place over some question of language. Especially as I had a preface to write.

I

Tarnation! Was this civvy going to make me wait any longer like that, me who knew the days when they sawed legs off without anesthesia. My extraordinary longevity had allowed me, in fact, to travel the long road that goes from Arcole to Moscow and from Magenta to Reischschoffen to end up at the Avenue de Tourville, and to see along the way some of these majors from Marjolin up to Nélaton.[1] It was precisely one of these gentlemen that I had come to consult, for headaches.

After saluting in military fashion, the doc stood to attention to inquire about my case, which I explained to him by means of some drawings that I sketched upon his wall, for as the *petit tondu*[2] said, a picture is worth a thousand words.

My explanations were certainly quite clear, because, taking a handsaw, he removed a shaving of my head, which he carefully examined.

"There're worms in there," he said, "better replace it with an ebony one."

"But I'd look like a negro," I cried.

"Well then," he replied. "I see what you need. You need tranquilizers."

"Say papa, what's the meussieu gonna do to me?"

"But nothing, my boy, nothing."

"Then, if the m'sieu's not doing anything to me why'd you take me to see 'im?"

"Because you're in pain, my boy, you're in pain."

"Say papa you know that better than me?"

He was about to slap me, when a guy comes in. Papa calls him doctor.

"So then, what seems to be the matter with this boy?"

"He's got a headache doctor."

"Perhaps he's working too hard."

"Him? A dunce!"

That there's unfair, I'm no dunce, so I stick my tongue out at my papa.

The doctor looks at it and he says:

"I see what it is, he needs tranquilizers."

II

The doc gave me an appointment, I said to myself, Great! I'm not going to have to wait.

I get there; fifteen people. I wasn't happy. Luckily there were some magazines there. I look at the pictures. Twelve people. I do the crosswords. Eight people. I do the bridge problem, but as I don't know how to play bridge, it's a bit tricky.

Finally it's my turn.

I go in. The doc says to me: Take off your trousers.

"Oh! Excuse me," I go, "it's for a headache."

"Ah ah, a headache," he goes. "You have some *idées fixes?*"

"Yes. Fixed in my head."

"Can you localize the pain?"

Localize—what does he mean, localize? Yet another learned word to scare people.

"I'm going to examine you," he tells me.

"That won't be difficult," I tell him, and I open my mouth and I show him my wisdom tooth, the one in such bad shape.

He looks at it and he says to me:

"I see what it is. You need tranquilizers."

In all the endeavors made up to the present day to demonstrate that $2+2=4$, the wind's velocity has never been taken into account.

The addition of whole numbers is actually possible only in weather calm enough so that, once the first 2 is put down, it stays in place until one can set down the little cross, then the second 2, then the little wall on which one sits to think, and finally the result. The wind can then blow, two and two have made four.

Should the wind pick up, then you have the first number on the ground. Should one persist, the same thing will happen to the second. What, then, is the value of $\text{и} + \text{и}$? Current mathematics are not in a position to provide us with an answer.

Should the wind rage, then the first numeral blows away, as does the little cross and so on. But let us suppose that it dies down after the disappearance of the little cross, then one might be led to write out the absurdity $2=4$.

But the wind not only carries away, it also brings. The unit, a particularly light number that a breeze alone is enough to move, can in this manner land in an addition where it is not needed, without even the calculator's knowledge. It is this that the Russian mathematician Dostoyevsky intuited when he dared declare that he had a partiality for $2+2=5$.

The rules of decimal numeration also prove that the Hindus had probably more or less expressed our axiom unwittingly. The zero rolls with ease, it is sensitive to the slightest puff of air. Therefore one doesn't take it into account when it is placed to the left of a number: $02=2$, because the zero buggers off before the end of the operation. It only becomes significant on the right, because then the preceding numerals can hold it back and stop it from blowing away. One then has $20 \neq 2$, provided the wind doesn't blow more than several meters a second.

We shall now draw a few practical conclusions from these considerations; as soon as one fears atmospheric disturbances, it is good to give an aerodynamic form to one's addition. It is also recommended one write it out from the right to the left, starting as close as possible to the edge of the sheet of paper. If the wind makes the operation in progress slide, one can, almost always, catch hold of it before it reaches the margin. One will thus obtain, even with an equinoctial storm, results like this:

In a tobacco shop, rue de Bussy, at the time of the Petiot affair:[1]

. . . to great minds, great passions . . .

. . . gotta be happy . . .

. . . they're smarter but not happier . . .

. . . nasty things, extraordinary things don't occur to us. We drink, we eat, we work, we don't have the time . . .

. . . virtue gets you nothing, just pennies. Whereas vice . . .

. . . not smarter than us. We simply weren't directed that way . . .

. . . an idler isn't harmful when he's dirty. Incapable of doing bad because he's incapable of bearing the weight of life . . .

. . . when you've got everything you could want, you look for things that aren't natural. A tramp won't ever steal, because he stoops to asking . . .

In a bar on the pont de Neuilly:

(on my right): . . . a parenthesis[2] is like a door, it opens and it closes . . . there's loads of people who do all sorts of things . . .

(on my left): . . . it's like the fable of the lion, the fox, and the donkey.

(the one on the right): . . . maybe I'm crazy, but how do you prove that you're not normal . . . there're people who drink, gotta know your limits . . . I had sorrows, I tried to drown them, they always floated back up to the surface . . .

Seeing the colossal headlines of the newspapers announcing the death of Cerdan,[3] *a policeman exclaims:*

"All the same he's not a scientist."

* * *

At the counter of an all-night bistro on the Champs-Élysées. It is two a.m.:

Manager: Hello, you two-bit hood, monsieur desires a drink?

Customer: Vichy-menthe.

Manager: A Vichy-menthe for his little mug. Cough up.

Second customer: Hello, Roger.

Manager: Hello, my dear friend.

Second customer: What do you say to a game of 421?

Manager: Between suckers like us, that don't wash. If we had a third thief, I dare say we'd fleece 'im.

Second customer: I'm offended, Roger.

In the shadow of Saint-Germain-des-Prés.

At the corner of rue Jacob and rue Saint-Benoît, one old woman to another: I heard the angelus ring so I booted my customer out . . .

In the shadow of Saint-Germain-des-Prés (continuation).

Waiting for the bus. One young woman to another: yesterday I bought the *Grève des Forgerons*,[4] I'd already read it, but I wanted to reread it.

In the street. A woman:

"If it's nothing, it's not a big deal."

A taxi driver:

" 'Ignorance of the law is no excuse.' What about them? They have to consult the Dalloz.[5] As if we had the time to consult the Dalloz. Exams are all luck. When I passed my leaving certificate, I had a problem I knew how to do, a dictation with no tricky words, an essay on a subject I liked. I passed the written exam. It was all luck."

"You're being modest."

"For the oral, they give me a question on the Aude. I answer: it's a river. Ah, says the examiner, it's not a river, it's not a stream, it's a coastal river. So I say: the Aude is a little coastal river. The examiner was happy: it was all luck. And so on and so forth. Anyway, all their books, their brochures, how are we supposed to get all of that into our little heads?"

He has a missing hand, replaced by a glittering nickel-plated apparatus to shift gears.

At a counter on the rue du Bac:
    Customer: A *claquesin.*
    Barmaid: Hot or cold?
    Customer: Cold, but no draft.

Enter M., Mme. and the child who immediately hoists himself onto a stool.
    Barmaid: What'll it be?
    The father *(glancing questioningly at the mother):* Two glasses of white.
    The kid: And two grenadines for me.

The owner, still a young woman, of a bistro on the avenue de Neuilly:
    "Time flies so quick . . . You've hardly had time to realize y'were on the earth."

At the counter of one of the grimiest bistros of the place Pigalle, two down-and-outs make conversation:
    First down-and-out: I heard there's a play worth seeing: *The Three Musketeers.*
    Second down-and-out: Yeah. But look, a seat's six hundred francs.
    The waiter *(intervening):* Gone with the wind . . .

At a bistro counter, avenue de la Grande-Armée. A woman and two men. The woman must "be in the theater":
    "Would you believe," she says to one of the two men, "would you believe that someone had to tell me *Britannicus,* I'd forgotten it."
    And, in turn, she starts telling (correctly) the "story"; she gets to: Néron loves Junie who loves Britannicus.
    The man: It's always like that in Corneille.
    She: Corneille? Corneille? You're confusing me. It's not Corneille, it's Racine.
    The other man: Corneille or Racine, it's like the detective novels, there's no smut.

At a bistro counter, rue de Sèvres.

It's raining.

The barmaid to a customer: It'll make the lettuce grow, the cherries. Gotta think of others, my dear. Can't just think of the cobblestones of Paris.

The customer: Well then, for me, I'll have a cobblestone of Beaujolais.

On the 73 bus. A big fat woman and a guy sit next to me while continuing their conversation:

She: What a moralist. I've never seen such a thing.

He: The same hot air every night. He shows up with his bitch . . . *Then they fall silent, pensive.*

In a bar, avenue Georges V. A guy is on the phone:

"But, madame, it's a very expensive dog . . . but of course . . . two hundred thousand francs . . . a very beautiful breed . . . what breed? what breed? . . . it's a French dog, madame . . ."

And the cloakroom attendant to a speaker I cannot see:

"I'd like to lend my studio, but naturally at a good price."

An obese woman, out of breath, heaves herself onto the bus. Not too old for all that. Stumbling, she collapses onto a seat. She coughs, hacks, spits. To the woman accompanying her:

"I've got a good constitution. But I never overindulge. Without that, I wouldn't be in the good health I'm in now."

Before the Saint-Médard church. A little old lady to a little old man waiting for her:

"The priest's there. As for me, it's done, I confessed . . . three minutes . . ."

On the 73 bus, a guy:

"My grandmother said to me: do what you please, don't do anything, when you come to nothing you'll see."

On the 63 bus. Probably boarded at the Gare d'Austerlitz, an old countryman and his wife, in their Sunday best. He acts as a guide. When we cross the boulevard Saint-Michel, he says:

"The Boul' Mich'."

The conductor announces "rue du Bac." He:

"The great musician."

In the 43 bus. One lady in her thirties to another:

"I don't know how to be bored . . . I don't manage to get what I have to do done . . . I get up at eight . . . at seven-thirty . . . my shopping . . . lunch . . . you leave the table, it's two . . . so I lie down for a bit . . . and then it's evening . . . *(little laugh)*."

The same lady:

"He has an incredible memory."

The other lady:

"He must find that very useful."

A barman at the time of the prix Goncourt:

"That must be all the rage right now . . . You're not discouraged? . . . You, you see things from a literary point of view, me, from a psychological point of view. People aren't what they used to be. They have no more . . . I won't say moral life . . . but no more . . . interior . . . no more . . . *(big gesture)* . . . circulatory life . . ."

In the street:

"Tomorrow, I never come."

In the street:

"A year, that's not old."

On the 73 bus. Place de la Concorde, a lady shows the obelisk to another:

"You see that? Napoleon stole it from the Egyptians."

In a taxi. The driver:

"The other day some buddies said to me: Arsène, let's go to Mme Arthur's. Mme Arthur? Yes, we're going to see Coccinelle.[6] I say to them: What's Coccinelle? Naturally I knew: I read the papers. They say to me: it's a male who does striptize.[7] Believe me, monsieur, in a couple of years you'll be seeing the cops on the place de la Concorde in tutus. People say to me: you're a killjoy, a wet blanket. But we reflect the world! They're the ones who are. What kind of fares do we get? People who go to funerals or the guy in a hurry with his little briefcase and a tie inside it. He's rushing, he's rushing . . . a red light, he moans . . . And in the evening, he goes home with his head as big as that and still his tie in his little briefcase."

We arrive at the traffic circle of the Champs-Élysées, before the clumps of flowers around the fountains.

"That would make a nice Van Gogh, eh? But these days, it's Buffet[8] . . . corpses . . ."

Melanopyge was strolling along the Seine, an ancient book under his arm, when he encountered Aristenete, who was strolling along the Seine, an ancient book under his arm.[1]

MELANOPYGE: The object you clasp so preciously under your arm, dear Aristenete, would it not be a work devoted to etymology?

ARISTENETE: Nay, dear Melanopyge.

MELANOPYGE: Well, such is the one I carry under my axilla, but it refuses to provide me the answer to the question I asked it.

ARISTENETE: And what was this question, dear Melanopyge?

MELANOPYGE: Tell me, dear Aristenete, from whence comes the French expression "five aux cloques"? I know that it translates as "five to the blisters" and concerns the hour, but as to what its origin might be, I confess I am unable to see.

ARISTENETE: What a spirit of curiosity you display, O Melanopyge, and what intuition might I add, in asking me such a question! I am delighted to have an answer so as to prove to you that in the domain of the linguistic sciences, I am without equal.

MELANOPYGE: Who has ever contested it, dear Aristenete?

ARISTENETE: Indeed, no one. This expression, we shall find its underlying origins in the *tough* tuff (as the Irishman would say) of the unconscious, proliferating and autoselftrophic activities of the logos.

MELANOPYGE: Ah! Ah!

ARISTENETE: Before this descent into the Underworld, I shall prepare the terrain with some more superficial work and content myself with using only the resources of simple analogy. Is there not some similarity between the expression that concerns you, dear Melanopyge, and this one: "cinq années aux cerises"?

MELANOPYGE: "Five years to the cherries"? If there is a similarity, dear Aristenete, I must admit that I do not see it.

ARISTENETE: Really?

MELANOPYGE: Really.

ARISTENETE: Knit your brows, then, and try to see further than the end of your nose.

MELANOPYGE: I redouble my efforts and still see nothing.

ARISTENETE: Concentrate! Let us concentrate on the expression: "cinq ans aux cerises"!

MELANOPYGE: Well there, dear and great Aristenete, I ask you to be kind enough and find enough kindness to forgive my emotion, but I find myself . . .

ARISTENETE: Where do you find yourself?

MELANOPYGE: . . . sadly obliged to contradict you.

ARISTENETE: Might I have said, dear Melanopyge, might I have said something stupid?

MELANOPYGE: Certainly not, dear and great Aristenete, and never would I dare ruffle your feathers with the spurs of contradiction, but you see . . .

ARISTENETE: What shall I see?

MELANOPYGE: . . . you proposed we concentrate our intelligence, mine that is slender and yours that is sublime, to concentrate them, I say, on the prior expression: "cinq années aux cerises," and there you are, if I understood correctly, you want to uncover for me the meaning of this "cinq ans aux cerises" that is already something completely different. Is there not some anamorphosis there? For, as you revealed to me yourself, one day when we were strolling along the Seine, ancient books under our arms, there are a thousand nuances that vary from one word to another.

ARISTENETE: Ah, my poor Melanopyge, how well you display your still great debility in the handling of these much debated questions. You at once plunge into the semantic, structural, and verrucose marasmus of discontinuity. Do you not understand, then, and do you understand not and understand you not that I passed in this way continuously and smoothly from "années" to "ans" and from "ans" to the zero lexeme that uncovers itself in all its nudity in the expression "cinq aux cerises"?

MELANOPYGE: You should have given warning, dear Aristenete, for you traverse the lexicon with the nimbleness of an interstellar rocket like the veritable logonaut that you are.

ARISTENETE: Thank you, once again, my very dear Melanopyge, I shall then walk at your side, at your pedestrian pace.

MELANOPYGE: Thank you, dear and great Aristenete.

ARISTENETE: Not at all. I return, then, to my "cinq aux cerises." For one who has some intuition of these things . . .

MELANOPYGE: And you have it, dear Aristenete.

ARISTENETE: . . . it is first necessary to detect the ambiguity of this drupe that, on the one hand, presents itself in a guileless and spring-like aura and, on the other, as synonymous with that type of cherry the French call a "guigne," thus synonymous with "guignon," which indicates rotten luck, *ergo* with misfortune, from which the apotropaic passage to "cloques," which possess the same ambiguity, since these "cloques" refer to the salutary effects of sunbathing as well as to the baleful ones of the illness that attacks the leaves of the peach tree and to the waste that is removed from wheat through cleaning. Such is the sense, finally, of the expression "five aux clo-ques" of which you were just inquiring.

MELANOPYGE: But "five" dear Aristenete . . .

ARISTENETE: Owing to the Channel Tunnel, see . . .

MELANOPYGE: Thank you, thank you, dear and great Aristenete, all that is now lucid and as the Saint-Clotilde belfry is ringing the fifth hour, will you permit me to offer you a cup of tea?

THE WAITRESS: Milk or lemon?

Cosmophilia

It takes an incredible boor, of course, to screw the dawn. Around the middle of the day, such a thing can be thought and done without wrinkling one's brow, but at the first squirt of sun, everything's broincy. The dawn obviously withers early. She flexes her bellebows, exposes her blue, attaches her zeros, cultivates her seed, coughs from the whip, turns gray. On the stroke of a little after noon, it's taken by an excess of surprise and above all by reprieve, but it's a bit of a severe casion, taken apart, as it were, not very commendable. The weather sags and supports the mixture above it. One goffers, one frothals, one bleeds and the moon appears in the unbroken violet of the soft green sky of the fin de six with its aftereffect of pompous undefined cloud-cubes. Then falls and drops the gloam. The same obtains the other and the night erects itself with a compliant calm. The stars prickle. The comet combs. The nebula freezes. There's nothing left but the unpleasant drowsiness to shut one's eyes by, with the calm of the sages.

Dialogue between Ogres

"Dragomir, did you put flesh pâté into the celery soup?"

"Yes, Minouchka, and what's more, human flesh."

"Manflesh, Dragomir, or woman—or better yet, child?"

"Just human flesh, Minouchka."

"What do you mean, Dragomir?"

"I mean earflesh, Minouchka."

"It's true, Dragomir: you are from Auvergne. Ex audiente nux."[1]

Articles

Q.—Tell me about articles.

A.—There are definite articles, indefinite articles, and household articles.

Q.—Tell me about household articles.

A.—Household articles are in the hands of housewives the way petroleum is in the hands of smalltime investors.

Q.—Tell me about smalltime investors.

A.—Smalltime investors are not an export article.

Q.—Why didn't you cite export articles just now?

A.—Because they belong to indefinite articles.

Q.—Are there other indefinite articles?

A.—Yes. The article of death.

Q.—Cite some definite articles.

A.—Again, the article of death.

Q.—Give me your general impression of articles.

A.—Pretty favorable.

Tit and Tat

They were each speaking two different languages, agglutinative languages with bitter roots, and at first that didn't bother them. Moreover, the rolled words in their rocky inlets spread mauve reflections, but little information. They tried various categories, faux nemes, pure verbs, clicks, moos: every time some eggs of sumethin' else hatched under their words.

It was completely baffling.

They were each speaking two different languages, agglutinative languages with bitter roots.

In the Letter

The shelter is colossal, within an a, for egzample, an o, an i—slim interior, of course, that of the i; but how certain it is, warm even, gemütlich.[2] That doesn't get you far on the road to fame, of course. Quite the contrary, you go all the more slowly. Oh, how many writers and editorneys

who had joyously left for far-off journeys
buried themselves in the interior of an i.[3]

If anyone is relaxed enough, they can choose something else: the aleph, the omega, the sampi.

Ah little flock, little flock, how you make us suffer.

The Haughties

If I were what I think I am, I would not be here making my bit of goose slave away in the ink, unsticking the ballpoint pen, cementing the scrapers, hardening the soft bits of bread. Where would I be, not here of course, I've already said so, letting my waterman rule my sergeant-major, capulating with some she-fur, training my park-curs, sojourning my elephants. You have to admit it, art has severe principles that go beyond the fame of the haughties. The haughties: those who believe they have a bit of it. They distinguish. They paradigm. They perpend. They sneakify. They gaudify. With my quill in the air, I say no and put three ens to my name and innumerable "o"s.[4]

Description of a Certain Joe Schmoe

A little thicker at the chin than at the corner of the spleen, that was the first thing that struck you when you didn't look at him too much from the side. Still old enough, though of a Venetian luster, he appeared to be bathed in more sweat than his boxing wanted. His eye fresh, but hung up, his look slightly stringy, ear at ease, nose green, mouth twitching, corners of the kennel decidedly too pronounced and Achilles tendon constantly at rest, his face thus made a shifty sound that the jolting curve of his shoulders was unable to glue up.

A chestnut brown detail corroborated his ventricles. The nourishment of his striking feature also fed the corn on his cob from which he suffered every seasoning. Nothing had ever been able to heal it, not even the dreary pension of an old tuna-meat pedant. His salad fermented over a slow heat between the schnozz and the ballast, but without loud singing so as not to awaken the eagle of the dulcimer, tough and quick tempered.

He would light up through auto-kept rotation of the pyrophor.

The ribs of his pen cap, made well enough to disgust a dandy, enveloped him from head to toe in a thin latticework of nags.

It was still no better.

Two fingers of fatigue, one of them too short and the other short enough, allowed him only the most sparing of waltz steps, but not always. To the right of the box of his biennial bone, there was nothing much to do, for him as well as for others, but to the left. He constantly heard himself talking, with a fillet of soil that sometimes descended to the hollow of the yew.

To every heart, he answered tails. That was the most caudal aspect of his behavior and the one that sometimes in his melancholy led him to screw down the asphalt of his first kernel. The passersby, disconcerted, hit the bull's-eye.

Line

It is here that Line was sentenced to death; sentenced Line was, to death, but, shortly before the execution, she contracts a serious illness, which delays her cinedeay execution.[5]

Heterogeneous Homophones

Few men keep abreast, all women have two.

He was smoking so much pot he was going to it.

Atop the Eiffel Tower, we got one of Paris.

While smoking a butt, he scratched his.

He drove away from the park because he couldn't.

Dressed in crêpe, she flipped several.

He turned red after his report card was.

Removing her veil, she descended into it.

To ensure that the drunkard wouldn't whine, they gave him some.

Being well bred, the child ate his buttered.

He made a call to the delivery room and learned that the baby wasn't born with one.

Jesus told Paul not to expect to find him in one.

The duck didn't and hit its head.

The Town of Ouste Is Actually Situated in the Lower Pyrenees

In France, in ancient times, three very distinct languages were spoken; in the first, north of the Loire, "oui" was said "oïl"; in the second, south of the Loire, "oui" was said "oc"; in the third, in the direction of Bayonne, "oui" was said "oust."

That is why some people still speak of "la langue oust bayonnaise."[6]

My Heart

Sometimes my heart is to the right, or even completely under my arm, as if it were growing hair. At times I feel it in my elbow, near the funny bone, I'm afraid it might take root there, I'd no longer be able to put them (my elbows) on the table, I prefer that it drop a little further down. Then I see it beating under my wrist, in the spot where palmists locate the line of longevity. Sometimes, it's rare, it reaches the ends of the fingers, the pulp. But it never stays there for long.

Then it comes back up, and, if I'm not careful, it travels unforeseen distances; I have to search for it and find it under a kidney, one of my nuts or the root of a hair.

That's why I'm going to the doctor.

O my heart, if only you'd be more quiet.[7]

Paralogies

That it gets ready, far from, the what has to be said, then the echoes that to the cock-a-doodle-dos[8] of an innate, but laughably long card the limits reply, reply. It's midnight. Some write, some dream. The ink flows through the fingers of the moon in its coaches of algebras. Next to, almost, thereabouts, the stopover point is announced by the blatant chimes of a five-franc piece. It's still noon. Time hasn't changed since the Silurian age. It's barely changed. Barely: just enough to no longer become a troglodyte.

The Grandmother

In the days when his grandmother was alive, he would say to her: you smell bad, you stink. Now that she's dead, he no longer knows what to say to her. He's not a vampire. When he goes for a walk in a cemetery, he behaves. He doesn't dig up the bodies, he knows his manners. He pisses to the right, to the left, he spits a bit, here and there; but that's all. He doesn't do more than that. He doesn't collect the faded flowers. He's content with murmuring things, with humming some *dies irae* to himself.

Sometimes the weather's nice.

But what did he do with his grandmother?

Little For Nothing

I was in the midst of writing when I got tripped up in a litotes. It lay on the ground, feeding on the new goo of blue hue, to embue, too, the zoo's poo-poo with dew, to truly view the flue, to rue, moo, coo, and even mew.

A Fish Passes By

I was drinking like a perch stuffing itself. A little more than steel, the sinker was melting the marble at the bottom of the sugar gulf where the fissures of a jostled coffee were dragging about, wounded. In the earth, in the earth, the filler perches. At the center, at the center, in the reversed tower of Babel that sits in the hollow of the foliage in the mine.

But a fish was passing by.

I was drinking like a spin-drying bleak. Choumeniga, Choumeniga, that's the name of the fisherman by the hearth, of the salamander fisherman with the bewitched felt hat, with tight-fisted feet, with limp fingers, and who barely agrees and who doesn't agree. The fishing line fries in the flames and the hook hops, no longer able to inhale the fresh air of the covered balconies.

But a fish passed by.

I was no longer drinking and in my parched state I no longer saw anything but the poker extinguishing itself in the distant glasses of beer, oh how distant they were, how distant. They're working on the Eiffel Tower and the carriage takes away the provincial lady with flabby thighs, and the cobblestones crunch under the fingers.

But a fish had passed by.

A great bronze wind was blowing hard enough to make one's nostrils burst. One was thus witnessing some factorizations, sanctimonious but corroborating. One never knows. The fire went out. One chokes. You run. No one passes by anymore.

Belgium Travels

They were hauling Belgium toward the shore of the Syrtes, but when they wanted to make it cross the Strait of Messina, the disaster took place. They had indeed succeeded in crossing the Rhine, the passes of the Alps then of the Apennines, they had steered clear of Capua and its delights, Sorrento and its lemonades, Paestum and its pediments, Calabria and its Calabrians, they truly had every reason to congratulate themselves; once in Sicily, it was no more than a game to take it up to the shore of the Syrtes.

It was then that the cables broke and that the piece of arable earth in question fell into the water. There were two million dead and five wounded, not counting the natives of Luxembourg.

The Enraged Sheep

He has a delicate nature. The slightest incident irritates him, but he behaves himself: he would kill if necessary. So many chipped days. Life fades like the dishes.[9]

The Hen with the Feline

This hen wanted a cat. She was a real hen, gallinaceous, a poultry hen, farmyard poultry, a farmyard of the Beauce, of the Beauce in France. This hen was named Amélie and her man, the rooster, his name was Clarion: a real schmuck. He scratched the mud while clucking, gesticulations meant to lead some fool under his feet so he could pork her. What *Amélie* wanted was a cat, a purring cat that she could pet and that would mew for its chow.

She would have had it fixed: no fuss.

But there it is: no cat consented. The melancholic Amélie wondered if she wouldn't choose her pet among some other species; she hesitated between the earthworm and homo sapiens.

Little Legs

The rooftops of Paris, lying on their backs,
with their little legs in the air.

The corps de ballet moves forward ardently,
on its little legs.

The worms of the tomb, with their little legs . . .

Don Juan, so tied down by his little legs . . .

He loses his temper, which escapes on its little legs.

He put seven league boots on his little legs.

After centuries of research, they finally noticed
that the isoceles triangle rectangle had little legs.

The little legs of the eyes, fixed in
their crow's feet . . .

It would have been a very ordinary pebble, if it
hadn't had little legs.

After buttering them up, the chef
sprinkled parmesan on his little legs.

As big as the Patagonians may be, mortal agony,
on its little legs . . .

The prima donna was singing at the top of her voice, on her little
legs.[10]

The Funereal Town

There's nothing around but the pasturage of the black-coats. Limp sheets have been hung on the candelabra of the municipal theater; nothing passes along the boulevards, except, perhaps, for the dust. The outskirts went out, shutting up its principles again. Perhaps they still sing at the street corners, the moulting mutes of yesterday. The roofs coil up, slowly. All the same, you can see the people parading by, but they're all numb, they stumble, they reach the corner over there and disappear.

A Skeptic's Profession of Infaith

I am incontinent because I live on an island and insect because I don't trust any.

The Ouiches

Ouiches are generally rectangular in shape, almost square, about twelve centimeters by eleven; certain deviant ones attain a length of almost twenty centimeters, but in these cases never exceed seven to eight in width. Their flesh takes on different colors in accordance with their species.

Gastronomes appreciate them in a very particular way. Sometimes they even order one hundred of them—per person.[11]

The Coachman of Corfu

The noble traveler is walking. He suspects nothing. He is searching, naively. He is searching for the beauty spot, the curious sight, the church, the military stone, the gorgonia, the metopes, the protomes, but a whip cracks, oh, the pretty little horse, but how skinny he is.

The coachman knows everything, he knows everything, he's the one that says so, and as he says so three times one has to believe him. The whip cracks, the haggard little horse trots, the noble traveler can rest assured, the coachman will show him the protopes, the metomes and everything. The noble traveler will see nothing at all, not even the hexastyle temple, the gymnasium or the summer garden.

The coachman goes everywhere, that is, everywhere there is no beauty spot, nor curious sight, nor pebble of definite antiquity. He prepares a picnic to eat on a beach of fine sand, far from gorgonias and idle fancies.

The noble traveler isn't happy.

Stern and silent, he passes before the coachman who will have to eat his picnic on his own.

1—Would you like to know the story of the three lively little peas?

    if yes, go to 4

    if no, go to 2.

2—Would you prefer that of the three tall slender beanpoles?

    if yes, go to 16

    if no, go to 3.

3—Would you prefer that of the three medium-sized mediocre bushes?

    if yes, go to 17

    if no, go to 21.

4—Once upon a time there were three little peas dressed in green who were sleeping soundly in their pod. Their oh so chubby faces were breathing through the holes of their nostrils and one could hear their sweet, harmonious snoring.

    if you prefer another description, go to 9

    if this one suits you, go to 5.

5—They were not dreaming. In fact, these little beings never dream.

    if you prefer that they dream, go to 6

    otherwise, go to 7.

6—They were dreaming. In fact, these little beings always dream and their nights secrete charming visions.

    if you want to know these dreams, go to 11

    if you're not particularly keen to, then go to 7.

7—Their dainty feet were dipped in warm socks and they wore black velvet gloves to bed.

    if you prefer gloves of a different color go to 8

    if this color suits you, go to 10.

8—They wore blue velvet gloves to bed.

    if you prefer gloves of a different color, go to 7

    if this color suits you, go to 10.

9—Once upon a time there were three little peas knocking about on the highways. When evening came, they quickly fell asleep, tired and weary.

    if you want to know the rest, go to 5

    if not, go to 21.

10—All three had the same dream, for they loved each other tenderly and, like good and proud thrins, always had similar dreams.

    if you want to know their dream, go to 11

    if not, go to 12.

11—They dreamed that they were getting their soup at the soup kitchen and that on opening their billies they discovered that it was vetch soup. They woke up, horrified.

    if you want to know why they woke up horrified, look up the word "vetch" in Webster's and let's not mention it again

    if you don't think it's worth going deeper into the matter, go to 12.

12—Opopoï![1] they cried as they opened their eyes. Opopoï! what sort of dream did we give birth to! Bad omen, said the first. Yah, said the second, you said it, I'm all sad now. Don't get in a tizzy, said the third, who was the craftiest of the three, this isn't something to get upset over, but something to understand, to cut a long story short, I'm going to analyze it for you.

    if you want to know the interpretation of this dream right away, go to 15

    if, on the contrary, you wish to know the reactions of the other two, go to 13.

13—That's a lot of hooey, said the first. Since when do you know how to analyze dreams. Yeah, since when? added the second.

    if you too would like to know since when, go to 14

    if not, go to 14 anyway, because you still won't know why.

14—Since when? cried the third. How should I know! The fact is I analyze them. You'll see!

    if you too want to see, go to 15

if not, go to 15 anyway, because you'll see nothing.

15—Well, let's see, then, said his brothers. I don't like your irony, he replied, and you won't know anything. Anyway, hasn't your feeling of horror dimmed during this rather lively conversation? Vanished, even? So what's the point of stirring up the quagmire of your papilionaceous unconscious? Let's go wash up at the fountain instead and greet this happy morning with hygiene and sacred euphoria! No sooner said than done: there they are slipping out of their pod, letting themselves gently roll along the ground and then, jogging, they merrily reach the theater of their ablutions.

if you want to know what happens at the theater of their ablutions, go to 16

if you would rather not, you go to 21.

16—Three big beanpoles were watching them.

if the three tall beanpoles displease you, go to 21

if they suit you, go to 18.

17—Three medium-sized mediocre bushes were watching them.

if the three medium-sized mediocre bushes displease you, go to 21

if they suit you, go to 18.

18—Finding themselves eyeballed in this way, the three nimble little peas who were very modest ran off.

if you want to know what they did next, go to 19

if you don't want to know, you go to 21.

19—They ran speedily to get back to their pod and, shutting it again behind them, went back to sleep.

if you would like to know the rest, go to 20

if you do not want to know, you go to 21.

20—There is no rest the story is over.

21—In that case, the story is also over.

Just as there are real human languages (French, Chinook, Burushaski, etc., just to name the best known) and imaginary human languages (the most famous of which is Psalmanazar's Formosan[1]), there exist real animal languages, (the language of crows, for instance) and imaginary animal languages (among which one can cite the language of Swift's Houyhnhnm and that of Edouard Chanal's sea lions). To these, we must add the dog language found in chapter 13 of *Sylvie and Bruno*.

Lewis Carroll provides a corpus of nine sentences that allows us to identify eighteen different words, whose meaning one can discover thanks to the translations he provides. (It is somewhat curious to note that Swift also reveals only seventeen words of Houyhnhnm to us—but leaves the meaning of five of them uncertain.)

From a phonetic point of view, dog language is comprised of two consonants (*B* and *H*), two semivowels (*Y* and *W*), and two vowels (*A* and *O*); at least if we confine ourselves to the transcription, but one could surmise that *ooh, oo* and *ow*, for example, designate different sounds. Be that as it may, the phonetics of the dog's language is even poorer than that of Tahitian (not mommy's little Tahitian, of course), which possesses five vowels and eleven consonants. One will also notice, still from a phonological point of view, that 66.66% of the words end in *ooh* and 11.11% in *ow*. *W*, on the other hand, is the most common initial letter (38.88%) followed by *H* (27.77%), *B* (16.66%), *Y* (11.11%) and *O* (5.55%). The grammar seems fairly close to Chinese; to the extent that one can assert such a thing with as restricted a material as this, there is no declension or conjugation. As for the syntax, it presents certain particularities typical of English—for example the interrogative turn of phrase, "Subject + to be + negation + adjective, to be + pronoun" also occurs in dog language.

The most striking fact is the existence of a verb "not to be": *Wooh*, different from the verb "to be": *Hah* (allow me to mention here that, in No. 1 of the *Subsidia Pataphysica*, I proposed appending to the French lexicon negative words formed by the prefixation of the letter *n* in the case of a term beginning with a vowel: thus "nêtre" [nobe] for "ne pas être" [not to be]. Hamlet would say: "Être ou nêtre, voilà la question" ["To be or to nobe, that is the question"]. Or yet: *"Hah. . . Wooh. . ."* ; but Lewis Carroll did not provide us with the equivalents of "that is "and"question" in dog language).

What relationships does this imaginary dog language have to real dog language? That is the question—and a tricky one at that. We are lacking serious data for resolving this problem; but one can establish such a comparison on a precise point: the proportion of monosyllabic words, disyllabic words, etc. François Rostand (*Développment de l'aboi chez un jeune chien, méthodes d'étude et premiers résultats [Development of the young dog's bark, methods of study and initial results]*, "Journal de psychologie normale et pathologique," April–June 1957) established that in its seventh month, a young pup utilizes

    37% monosyllables

    35% disyllables

    27% trisyllables

    1% tetrasyllables or higher.

One finds in Lewis Carroll:

    44.44% monosyllables

    44.44% disyllables

    11.11% trisyllables

    0 % tetrasyllables or higher.

These observable differences can be explained either by the fact that Lewis Carroll's subjects are adults, or by the Britishness of some and the Welshness of others.

For the sake of completeness, we bring the reader's attention to chapter 4 of *Sylvie and Bruno (Concluded)* where one can find the word *Bosh*, which in "Doggee" means "the same thing as in English," but pronounced (by the Dog-King) half like a *cough* and half like a *bark*.

We have not taken this nineteenth word of dog language into account; it seems Lewis Carroll did not seek to keep its phonological structure, which perhaps he had forgotten, in accordance with that of the terms cited in the first part.

At the beginning of this essay, allusion was made to Edouard Chanal; as this writer seems to me to be little known, this might be an opportune moment to provide some details about him.

Born in 1844, died at a date unknown (to me), a German instructor and then school inspector, he is the author of several guidebooks and scholarly works, and of two prize books both published by Gédalge: *Les Pensums du Père Bombyx [Father Bombyx's Chores]* (1898) and *Prisonnier dans un Dolmen ou la Journée d'un Métromane [The Dolmen's Captive or a Day in the Life of a Metromaniac]* (no date; subsequent to the *Pensums,* missing from the Bibliothèque Nationale), which we will look at first.

In the course of a picnic in the region of Nice, one of the members of the honorable society—a hunchbacked, provincial poet—enters into the crevice of a rock and is unable to extricate himself; workmen with picks, pickaxes, etc. have to be called for. While waiting for them, the picnic carries on and the hunchbacked, provincial poet (named Ambroise Mignon) is sentenced by his friends to 1. express himself only in verse; 2. engage in some technical feats; and so he has to compose:

a) some calligrammes (a glass, p. 80; the Royal spondyle, pp. 82-83);

b) a poem in set rhyme (p. 94) and on these same rhymes: an acrostic (p. 97), a double acrostic (p. 99) and a triple acrostic (on the initial letter, the hemistich and diagonally) (p. 102).

Meanwhile, one of the other members of the honorable society composes a Chinese comedy with a "gloomy conclusion" (ch. 6) and another an epic poem in prose identifying Napoleon with Jesus Christ (ch. 7, 9, 11, and 13): the Egyptian campaign is the flight into Egypt; the sermon on the Mount, the defeat of the Montagnards; St. Helena, Golgotha, etc.; it is also he—Napoleon—who deciphered the hieroglyphics, invented the lightning conductor and the steamship, etc.

Finally, Ambroise Mignon engages in some exercises in style; he gives several different translations of Heine's poem *The Grenadiers*:

1. literal (p. 155);

2. in octosyllables and conversational French (pp. 156–58):

They were all then having a ball,
Glasses in hand, France on her knees,
The Grand Army taking its fall—
The Emperor had just been seized!

3. in decasyllables and a more elevated style (pp. 161–63):

Then was described to them their tragic plight!
How dear France had been shattered and shaken,
How her army was put to dismal flight,
And how the Emperor had been taken!

4. in pentasyllables (pp. 166–70):

The news was blared out
France's pride was stained,
The Guard put to rout,
The Emperor chained.

5. in octosyllables, without using the letter *u* (pp. 173–74, "the exiled vowel"):

They heard tell the bitter story
How dear France was going to hell,
Her Grand Army's loss of glory,
Napoleon locked in a cell.

The rest of this work is of less interest (verse translations of German poems).

In the *Pensums du Père Bombyx*, one finds a double acrostic (p. 160), some reflections on rare rhymes (pp. 169 to 171) and some information on the language of sea lions, made up exclusively of vowels (p. 227). Examples:

Ouâ, â, â, Ouuïë!
Long live Gulliver! (p. 233)
Ouuïé, ouïouï
Gulliver, here is your good lunch (p. 241)
Ouïe, ouaïe, aïe
Gulliver, could misfortune have befallen you? (idem)

It was perhaps not inopportune to call the figure of Edouard Chanal to mind on the subject of Lewis Carroll. Both of them academics, and almost contemporaries, they also had in common a certain non-puerile and certainly not very educational notion of children's books.

I go to a mathematicians' luncheon. The first guest who arrives is carrying a cello. Although we are in one of the inner suburbs, we find ourselves before a brook with water lilies sprouting from it. One of the mathematicians present points out how Heraclitus was mistaken in saying that one never bathes in the same river twice: when one drinks a glass of water there are surely several molecules of H_2O that have already passed through our body. The others agree.

I run into an Arab and tell him about the death of a Spanish worker with whom he was acquainted. He isn't surprised, for this worker was working on a building site where an iron ball had fallen on his head. I approach the neighboring building site: the Seine has overrun the foundations. They've had to cut off the water.

My sister-in-law brings back the books I had lent her. I was unable to remember their titles. She is driving a little car with automatic transmission and complains of rheumatism.

I am in the country at the home of a doctor. He is grilling some eggplants and cutlets, which catch fire, then he plays the lute.

One of my friends is dead. Another of my friends whom I haven't seen in a long time goes to kiss him on the forehead. A third asks me the identity of a lady who is present. I tell him: "She's the head of manufacturing." He: "The head of manufacturing's wife?"—"No," I say to him, "*the* head of manufacturing." He goes to shake her hand.

The butcher's wife writes me a letter, asking me to leave the shutters *à l'italienne.* I wonder why and what she means.

I am in a little town whose topography is unfamiliar to me. I try to follow the same route as the day before. I venture, however, down a narrow alley whose buildings seem abandoned. There is a barbershop there without barber or clients. I wonder what he could have been thinking to have set up shop in a spot with so little traffic. Leaving this alley I see a fat lady in pants who is walking a cat at the end of a long leash and who is accompanied by a Siberian spitz.

I enter a church that is still adorned with a traditional altar. On a sheet of commercial-sized paper posted on the confessional there is a list of the members of the brotherhood of Saint Rose. I read it carefully. Then I examine with equal care the foot of a Romanesque column decorated with a hare and a snail. As I am about to leave, a priest in a cassock enters. I ask him what the Saint Rose brotherhood is. He explains it to me, but I have only retained a confused recollection of his explanations concerning the brotherhood (it's a matter of consecrated bread . . . of masses spoken . . .); as to the saint, he stresses that it is not the Saint Rose of Lima, but a local saint.

A little later, I find myself in an isolated hamlet. There is a church there that is associated with the Hôtel de Sens in Paris. The neighboring farmer has lent the key so that it can be visited. He arrives bare-chested, accompanied by his wife, who is wearing shorts. Before us there is a pond; the ducks and drakes are going to sleep for it is very late. The moon is almost full.

I ask in a cafe where the Saint-Baudel chapel is located. No one knows except for the proprietress, who shows me the way. I find it without difficulty. Inside I see two nearly nude boys on mattresses; pennants of the Jeune Garde on the walls, but the sixteenth century paintings that I was expecting to find are still on the ceiling.

* * *

In an absolutely deserted village, a countryman in the main square is trying to make a parachute-shaped kite rise up into the air.

I have rented a house, which I leave in order to go into the garden. I am surprised to find a lady there in the midst of shelling peas. She is settled on a rocking chair: "Come over to our side, then." I apologize, stammering, and close the door behind me.

I see a poster kept under glass over a grave. It is the speech made by a miller in 1896; a speech that he had printed: a eulogy to his mother who died at the age of eighty-two. He is the third of eighteen children. The word "fatal" is in the text, and others of the same sort.

I go into the neighboring church, which has been restored with shiny exposed beams and handrails with neon lighting. Two little gothic carved figures, however, remain.

I go out and again find myself in the cemetery. They have grouped together the graves of those who died in the war. There are four of them. The crosses that surmount the graves and the chains that join them together are in wrought iron of a peculiar style.

I go to reread the miller's speech.

Some parents visit Saint-Benoît with their little girl. I am looking attentively at the capitals when the father says to me (addressing me familiarly): "Explain to her what mass is." I look at the little girl. She must be six years old. I ask: "Has she received a Christian upbringing?" "No," he replies. I feel rather muddled and keep quiet while the father launches into explanations that the little girl listens to with round eyes. The mother smiles. She has purchased some cakes: they are good, it seems, at Saint-Benoît-sur-Loire.

Seated at a table on the terrace in a little provincial town, I am looking at the statue of a physicist and, in spite of the twilight that is transforming into night, am trying to make out the inscriptions on the pedestal. All of a sudden, sirens. People come to the windows. Some time passes. The shutters close again. There are no more onlookers when the fire engine passes by. Then an individual suddenly appears from the darkness, whose face reminds me of that of a mulish alcoholic of Depot 24 during the phony war. He comes up to me and holds his hand out, calling me master.

Of course none of these dreams are any more real than they are invented. They are simply minor incidents taken from wakened life. A minimal effort of rhetoric seemed sufficient to give them a dreamlike aspect.

That's all I wanted to say.

Translator's Introduction

1. Queneau kept a record of everything he read from his teenage years to his death. One can peruse the voracity of his reading appetite in two volumes recently published: Florence Géhéniau, ed., *Queneau analphabète*, ([Brussels?]: F. Géhéniau, 1992).

2. Some have been previously translated and published in various, mostly out-of-print, anthologies. I have included references to these in the notes.

3. These are presented by Claude Debon in "Le statut de la nouvelle dans l'œuvre de Queneau" in Bernard Alluin and Yves Baudelle, eds., *La Nouvelle II: nouvelles et nouvellistes au XXe siècle* (Villneuve-d'Acq: Presses Universitaires de Lille, 1992).

4. Collège de 'Pataphysique, *The True, the Good, the Beautiful: an Elementary Chrestomathy of 'Pataphysics*, trans. Andrew Hugill (London: Atlas Press, 1993), p. 11.

5. Trans. Alfred Cismaru in his *Boris Vian* (New York: Twayne Publishers, 1974), p. 24.

6. Cismaru, *Boris Vian*.

7. Cismaru, *Boris Vian*, p. 25.

8. René Daumal, *The Powers of the Word*, trans. Mark Polizzotti (San Francisco: City Lights, 1991), p. 19. Daumal makes for a very interesting counterpart to Queneau: both managed to unite the Eastern metaphysics of René Guenon with a deadpan espousal of 'Pataphysics.

9. Raymond Queneau, *Journaux*, ed. Anne Isabelle Queneau (Paris: Gallimard, 1996), p. 883. The College's homosexual roots were yet another point of opposition (even if unintended) to Breton and the Surrealists, whose antipathy to such forms of sexuality is well known. Queneau had been one of the exceptions, and his tolerance on the issue is documented in the first of the Surrealists' discussions on sexuality.

10. See Jane Alison Hale, *The Lyric Encyclopedia of Raymond Queneau* (Ann Arbor: University of Michigan Press, 1989), p. 27.

11. Alastair Brotchie, ed., *A True History of the College of 'Pataphysics*, trans. Paul Edwards (London: Atlas Press, 1995), p. 35.

12. Queneau, *Journaux*, p. 68.

13. Collège de 'Pataphysique, *The True, the Good, the Beautiful*, trans. Hugill, p. 7, translation modified.

14. Collège de 'Pataphysique, *The True, the Good, the Beautiful*, trans. Hugill, p. 12.

15. Lao Tsu, *Tao Te Ching*, trans. Gia-Fu Feng and Jane English (New York: Vintage, 1989), p. 5, 39.

16. Daumal, *Powers of the Word*, p. 15. The College's obscured outlook on the subject is evident in their ABC *of Accepted Ideas*, written by Georges Petitfaux: in the entry for "humor," members are advised to refrain from any comments on the subject.

17. *The Review of Contemporary Fiction* 17, 3 (fall 1997), p. 43.

18. Queneau, *Journaux*, pp. 712, 888.

19. "L'Humour et ses victimes": an essay that was perhaps one of the few of the Parisian thirties to suggest that the fabular tradition was not only a viable literary form, but also the conveyor of "true" humor.

20. Constantin Toloudis, *Rewriting Greece: Queneau and the Agony of Presence* (New York: Peter Lang, 1995), pp. 44–45.

21. *Review of Contemporary Fiction* (fall 1997), p. 24.

22. Queneau, *Journaux*, p. 67.

23. Claude Simonnet, *Queneau dechiffré (notes sur "Le Chiendent")* (Paris: Julliard [1962]), p. 102. My translation is from the French of this edition.

24. Simonnet, *Queneau dechiffré*.

25. Queneau, *Journaux*, p. 261.

26. Raymond Queneau, *Le Voyage en Grèce* (Paris: Gallimard, 1973), p. 103.

27. Allen Thiher, *Raymond Queneau* (Boston: Twayne, 1985), p. 76.

28. Hale, *Lyric Encyclopedia*, p. 5.

29. Daumal, *Powers of the Word*, p. 15.

30. Daumal, *Powers of the Word*, p. 16.

31. Daumal, *Powers of the Word*, p. 18.

Preface

Michel Leiris, as well as being a fellow member of the College of 'Pataphysics, was also, according to Jean Quéval (in *Prospice* no. 8 [1978]), one of only three people who used the familiar form of address with Queneau (the other two being Queneau's fellow Oulipians, Jean Lescure and François Le Lionnais).

1. A strange allusion for Leiris to make, given that Queneau attacked this idea of "black humor" in a review of Breton's *Anthology of Black Humor* in 1945 (an article reprinted in "Lectures pour un front" in *Batons, chiffres et lettres*). Queneau, who had already been disturbed by the strains of sadism running through the pulp fiction of the time, claimed Nazism to be an example of "black humor" put into practice.

Destiny

Written in 1922, when the author was still a teenager, "Destinée" never saw print before Gallimard published this collection in 1981. Queneau's recently published journals offer an impression of his state of mind at this time: "excruciating moral depression, thoughts of suicide, etc. (I can only imagine three ends: death, the most abominable mediocrity, exile to distant regions). Unsociable: I've no friends (girlfriends even less!)." Soon after, he writes: "I've started a novel (?) entitled either

Christian Stobel, or *Le Comité des Hommes Moyens* [The Committee of Average Men]"
but soon writes (March 31): "All that's of no interest"—a sentiment that more or less
ends this tale. (Queneau, *Journaux,* pp. 98–99).

As well as being something of a portrait of the author as a young man, the story's
title presents what would become one of Queneau's preponderant themes. What
Leiris describes as Queneau's fundamental abhorrence of the exotic is closely linked
to his attitudes toward chance and fate. The apparent acts of chance and freedom so
dear to the surrealists are negated throughout Queneau's works up to his last novel,
The Flight of Icarus, in which a character's Pirandellian escape from the confines of an
unfinished novel in itself becomes an act anticipated by his author. Destinies are always foreseen and fulfilled in Queneau's universe: Alfred of *The Last Days* fulfills his
goal of winning back his father's fortune (an act that ultimately changes nothing in
his life) and concludes the book by describing the day when the universe itself will
fulfill its destiny and vanish; the essential conflict of *Odile* involves Roland Travy sub-
mitting to the destiny of "banal" love and happiness he sees as imposed upon him.
The severity of this conflict, this act of submission, can be seen in Queneau's heated
remarks during the fifth session of the Surrealist discussions on sexuality: to Max
Ernst's question, "do you believe there is a woman who is your destiny," Queneau's
replies are, according to Breton, "typically counter-revolutionary and typically anti-
love." After Queneau finally states that he "can conceive of love apart from this destiny that people are trying to impose on me," Breton decides the discussion to be "a
question of vocabulary." (José Pierre, ed., *Investigating Sex: Surrealist Research 1928–1932,*
trans. Malcolm Imrie [London: Verso, 1992], pp. 75–79). The fact that Queneau rein-
troduces the question in the following session, though, indicates that he took such
vocabulary pretty seriously.

Alain Calame sees the "enigmatic metaphysician" of section 3 as being René
Guénon, an author Queneau had just read for the first time a few months earlier in
December of 1921, and whom he was to reread throughout the rest of his life.
Calame proposes reading this story in the light of Guénon's *Introduction générale à
l'étude des doctrines Hindoues.*

The prose betokens an early Surrealist influence in its style, even though he wasn't
to officially join the group for another couple of years. Portions of sections 3 and 4
in particular read like attempts at the sort of automatic style exemplified by Breton
and Soupault's *The Magnetic Fields,* which appeared in *Littérature* in 1919 (a journal to
which Queneau began to subscribe the year prior to the composition of this text).

As to Christian Stobel's name, his given name could have arisen from the religious
concerns of Guénon; "Stobel," though, might derive from the English "stob," which
means a stake or post: something unmoving or anchored in the midst of travels (that
which distinguishes a "destiny" from a "destination"). Stobel already betokens one of
the primary attributes of the future pataphysician: imperturbability.

PREVIOUS TRANSLATIONS:
"Destiny," translated by Brigitte Lambert, in *Atlas Anthology III,* Alastair Brotchie and
Malcolm Green, eds. (London: Atlas Press, 1985).

"Destiny," translated by Krzysztof Fijalkowski and Michael Richardson, in *The Dedalus Book of Surrealism: The Identity of Things*, Michael Richardson, ed. (Sawtry: Dedalus, 1993).

1. The explanation for the title of this section can be found in Queneau's autobiographical novel, *The Last Days*, in which he describes the development of Vincent Tuquedenne's cinematic taste for American comedies at the end of 1922, and for one Mack Sennett film in particular, "located on a beach and enlivened by bathing beauty girls with a grace that no one in those days could have suspected of one day becoming a little obsolete. Solitary, melancholy and ingenuous, he watched these incarnations of luxury and voluptuousness disporting themselves on the shores of the Pacific Ocean. And without being chaste, he was still a virgin. He liked images and respected shadows." (*The Last Days*, trans. Barbara Wright [Normal IL: Dalkey Archive Press, 1990], p. 175.)

Queneau reworked the second paragraph of this section a couple of years later into one of his unpublished texts from his Surrealist period (see [Il ne s'agit plus de rire! . . .] in *Œuvres complètes I*, ed. Claude Debon [Paris: Gallimard, 1989], p. 1003). This brief elegy to the cinema was followed, more than forty-five years later, by his poem in *Fendre les flots*: "The Bathing Beauty Girls."

When the Mind . . .

"Lorsque l'esprit" was written around 1928–29, and published in June 1929 in a special issue of *Variétés* devoted to Surrealism. It is one of the few texts by Queneau to be printed under the auspices of this movement, as he would soon break with André Breton in January of 1930. It would later be claimed and republished by the College of 'Pataphysics, with an added preface by Oktav Votka, as the inaugural volume of their "Collection Q." This republication fell under the sign of the Cold Solid Sun on 29 Tatane 82 (somewhere between 10–11 August 1955, as the 29th is a "hunyadi," one of the College's imaginary days intended to bring the number of days of each of the thirteen pataphysical months to a prime number). Indeed, the alternative science it proposes is very much in the style of Alfred Jarry's brand of science fiction, recalling René Daumal's declaration (also in 1928–29): "Pataphysics will make mockery of science, and be more educational." (*The Powers of the Word*, trans. Polizzotti, p. 19). But this piece also seems to demonstrate a cognizance of the "literary lunatics" (or "heteroclites"), whom Queneau would be researching over the next few years (research that would be eventually incorporated into his 1937 novel, *Children of Clay*). Of the four divisions of literary lunacy made by the character Chambernac in this novel, "When the Mind . . ." would fall under THE WORLD: "the various cosmologies, cosmographies, and aberrant systems of physics" [*Children of Clay*, trans. Madeleine Velguth [Los Angeles: Sun & Moon, 1998], p. 173]. This text probably owes a particular debt to one of Queneau's favored heteroclites, Pierre Roux, whose belief in an excremental sun made a strong impression on him.

"When the Spirit . . . ," partial translation by Robert Motherwell, Bernard Karpel and Arthur A. Cohen, in *The Autobiography of Surrealism*, Marcel Jean, ed. (New York: Viking, 1980).

1. The format of this series was very irregular, each issue taking on a different physical shape. The name "Q" apparently derives not from Queneau's name, but from its homophone, "cul" (ass).

2. Bosse-de-Nage is Dr. Faustroll's cabin boy throughout his journeys in Alfred Jarry's *Exploits and Opinions of Dr. Faustroll, Pataphysician*, trans. Simon Watson Taylor (Boston: Exact Change, 1996); he is a dogfaced baboon whose vocabulary consists of the exclamation "Ha ha." A starosta is a noble in Poland, which is to say, in pataphysical parlance (and as Jarry says in his introduction to *Ubu Roi*), "nowhere." Poland had no autonomy at the end of the nineteenth century.

3. J.-H. Sainmont, Proveditor General, Assistant, and Rogatory, was, along with Oktav Votka and His Magnificence Dr. Sandomir, one of the cofounders of the College of 'Pataphysics. After some shady goings-on within the College's structure at the time of Sandomir's decline, Sainmont resigned and was soon committed to an asylum.

4. Oktav Votka (Joseph Feldman) was a cofounder of the College of 'Pataphysics; according to pataphysical lore, it was in a conversation between him and Maurice Saillet in "La Maison des Amis des Livres" that the words "Collège de 'Pataphysique" were first uttered on 22 Palotin 75 (11 May 1948). He died 14 Décervelage 87 (11 December 1960).

5. One can see the "anticipatory plagiarism" the College of 'Pataphysics must have seen in this observation; compare it, for example, to the comment made years later by the College's R. Urbain Le Hennuyeux: "the principle of distinctions does not reside in what we do, but in the way in which we do it. It is not 'subject-matter' which is classified, but attitudes, operations, structures developed by those who 'deal with' these 'matters.'" (Collège de 'Pataphysique, *The True, the Good, the Beautiful*, trans. Hugill, p. 14.)

6. For a cosmological antecedent, one can compare this observation to those of Renault de Bécourt, one of Queneau's heteroclite discoveries, who claimed, among other things, that "the world is an egg whose air is the white and the terrestrial globe the yoke." (*Children of Clay*, trans. Velguth, p. 178) Queneau had also written in the early thirties "Le symbolisme du soleil" (The symbolism of the sun), an essay that drew anthropological links between the sun, the egg, maternity, and excrement. He there points out that in Finnish mythology, it is the sun that is the yolk of the world's egg.

A Bit of Glory

"La Petite Gloire" was published posthumously in 1979 in *Temps mêlés: Documents Queneau* no. 150+4 (May 1979), but was written sometime in the 1930s. It bears even more obvious relations than "When the Mind . . ." to Queneau's research on unknown and unrecognized nineteenth-century French authors; in this case, however, he takes on the perspective of one of his subjects. Instead of portraying himself seeking out Chambernac's research, as he did in *Children of Clay*, the "heteroclite" author here seeks out the scholar. Even so, M. G. still fits Chambernac's definition: "madness," as he comes to realize, "is the self-deification of an individual entity in which no collective entity will recognize itself" (*Children of Clay*, trans. Velguth, p. 396); a definition that, in Chambernac's case, ultimately applies to both the writer and the scholar. This story's scholar avoids the trap through a nearly perfect pataphysical laissez-faire, which does not, however, spare him an untimely end.

Queneau's interest in these cases of unknown writers ended up not so much literary as anthropological. He concluded his years of research with an attack on the romantic association made between the ideas of genius and nonrecognition in a 1939 article, "Des génies méconnus" [Unrecognized geniuses]: "On the contrary, it is because they don't have genius that 'literary madmen' are always unrecognized" (*Le Voyage en Grèce*, p. 164 n.2).

Queneau probably refocused on this condition of being unrecognized. From 1932 to 1939, he had attended Alexandre Kojève's seminal lectures on Hegel, in the course of which Kojève rooted Hegel's master/slave dialectic in a fight to the death for recognition: "It is only by being 'recognized' by another, by many others, or—in the extreme—by all others, that a human being is really human, for himself as well as others" (*Introduction to the Reading of Hegel*, trans. James H. Nichols Jr. [Ithaca: Cornell University Press, 1980], p. 9). In killing the scholar, the only individual capable of recognizing him, M. G.'s last act collapses this dialectic and seals his destiny. There is something in the ending of this story that recalls the character of Tolut in *The Last Days*, who decides that leaving a ghost behind is the only solution to a failed life and a bad conscience—a conscience that is not acknowledged or recognized by anyone other than himself and thus unsatisfied by the punishment he feels he deserves. An unrecognized consciousness, too caught in its own megalomania to even be capable of recognizing another: perhaps this would be the true literary ghost?

In Queneau's preface to the French edition of William Faulkner's novel, *Mosquitoes*, he asks: "Is the writer, even when dead, such a nothingness that his work can inscribe itself into human 'culture' without its original significance of being the work OF someone?" (quoted by Claude Simonnet in *Queneau déchiffré*, p. 117). One might reverse the sentiment for this story: Is the work, even when unread, such a nothingness that its writer can fade from human "culture" without his original significance of being the author OF something?

Panic

"Panique" was written in 1934 and possibly published the same year (although the earliest printing I have been able to locate is in *Mesures* 15, 1 (15 January 1939). It was later published by Éditions de Minuit with "Green with Fright" and "Dino" as the ternary *Une Trouille verte*. In that volume, it is preceded by "Dino," and, indeed, an unseen (invisible?) pup starts "Panic" off on a scatological note.

As with its two companion pieces, an inexplicable fear lies at the root of this story, an undefinable "impression." But an impression of what? That 30-6=24? The numerology is rather specific, from the room numbers to the hours to the 24 hour span of time that the story covers. Queneau had most likely completed his thirtieth year when writing this story (the cost of a room for one night); the Holy Alliance alluded to would have taken place about 120 years before that (120÷4=30); 30+6=36 (or 6x6); 24=6x4. But perhaps what is important to keep in mind is that "impression" can also signify "pattern" in French, and as Christopher Shorley says in his study on Queneau: "the very presence of pattern, rather than its possible meaning, is sometimes what counts the most" (*Queneau's Fiction: An Introductory Study* [New York: Cambridge University Press, 1985], p. 61).

PREVIOUS TRANSLATION:
"Panic," translated by Barbara Wright in *French Writing Today*, Simon Watson Taylor, ed. (New York: Grove Press, 1969).

A Young Frenchman
"Un Jeune Français nommé Untel, I, II" was written in 1935 and published in an English translation in *365 Days* (see below), under the titles "Afternoon of Crime" (24 June) and "After the Races" (3 July). The dates of the pieces come from the concept behind *365 Days*: the editors had commissioned short stories of roughly three hundred words each to correspond to every day of 1934, using newspaper articles from each day as starting points. Other French authors who collaborated included Michel Leiris, Georges Sadoul, and Jacques Baron. Queneau, however, was one of several authors who did not use newspaper articles as the basis for their stories.

The original French texts had long been presumed lost, and were found only after Jean Queval had retranslated them into French. The original versions appeared in *Contes et propos*.

"So-and-so," a defiant nobody, bears some relation to the earlier Stobel, both in certain autobiographical attributes (such as his predilection for mathematics), and in his Dadaist character.

PREVIOUS TRANSLATION:
"Deux Contes," translated by Laurence Vail in *365 Days*, Kay Boyle, Laurence Vail, and Nina Conarain, eds. (New York: Harcourt, Brace, 1936).

Dino
Written sometime in the 1930s and published in *Messages* no. 2 (1942), "Dino" was then reprinted in *Une Trouille verte* with "Green with Fright" and "Panic." As Leiris mentions in his preface, the dog ("chien") is the materialistic half of Queneau's "delicate etymology" (the other being the idealism of the oak tree, "chêne," hence the title of his autobiographical "novel in verse," *Chêne et chien*); Queneau traced both to two Norman French words, "quêne" [oak] and "quenet/quenot" [dog]. Opposed to the "great and noble" oak, "The dog is dog to a tee, / he's cynical, indelicate" (see Madeleine Velguth's translation, *Raymond Queneau's "Chêne et chien"* [New York: Peter Lang, 1995], p. 65).

Dino is perhaps Queneau's best-known dog, if only for the fact that he reappears, more or less, in *At the Forest's Edge*. Their similarities are notable: both fond of dining rooms and sugar, they also display acts of invisibility to everyone but their owners and provide a companionship to offset the melancholy that always laces the absurdity of Queneau's work.

PREVIOUS TRANSLATION:
"Dino," translated by Barbara Wright in *French Writing Today*, Simon Watson Taylor, ed. (New York: Grove Press, 1969).

At the Forest's Edge

"À la limite de la forêt" was written in 1940 and published on its own by Éditions Fontaine in 1947 in their "L'Âge d'or" collection. As Jacques Bens points out in the one essay devoted to this story (to be found in "À la limite d'un roman," *Europe* nos. 650–51 [June–July 1983]), Queneau was most likely working on *Les Temps mêlés* at this time (which would eventually develop into the second part of *Saint Glinglin*).

It is difficult to construe what Queneau might have intended to do with this abandoned novel; its incompletion aside, the bizarre acts and attitudes of the characters leave much to the imagination. Bens sees certitude as the one theme linking all these characters: Desnouettes firmly believes in a talking ape but refuses to believe in the possibility of a talking dog; and Gubernatis himself witnesses this dog speaking but refuses to believe his eyes and calmly attributes other causes to Dino's vocal ability.

Christopher Shorley believes Queneau is playing on the form of the German *Novelle*, with the presence of a "Doppelgänger" and its atmosphere of mystery. A characteristic of this form particularly in keeping with Queneau is what E. K. Bennett describes as an element of the unusual or fantastic occurring within the realm of reality, but the comparison might otherwise be a little strained (*A History of the German Novelle* [Cambridge: Cambridge University Press, 1961]). Claude Debon sees the monkey-visitor, with his ability to change form, as possibly embodying the devil, but this claim also has little to support it—the tale could just as easily, given its talking animals and somewhat bestial Blandi, read like a fairy-tale account of evolution ("Le statut de la nouvelle," in *La Nouvelle II*).

Whatever Queneau's intentions were on the whole, my own suspicion is that Amédée Gubernatis's given name derives from that of Amédée Fleurissoire, the victim of Lafcadio's "acte gratuit" in André Gide's *Lafcadio's Adventures*, (one of the novels Queneau reread most frequently: Shorley sees Fleurissoire's train journey in that novel reflected in Queneau's *The Sunday of Life*; *Queneau's Fiction*, p. 96). Their points in common, though, are inverted: Queneau's character appears to be riddled with certainty and makes no room for the sort of unmotivated action or crime that would be at obvious odds with the author's sensibilities; rather than succumb to the wiles of a sudden bed partner (as does the chaste Fleurissoire), Gubernatis chases her out of his room; and as the reader will discover, Fleurissoire's confused Catholic secret mission against the Freemasons is at odds with the Freemason Gubernatis's (suspiciously) banal and out-of-season walking tour to the church of Gougougnac. Jacques

Bens is most likely right to suspect that Queneau had more up his sleeve than sightseeing to sustain what was to be a novel-length plot ("À la limite d'un roman").

PREVIOUS TRANSLATION:
"At the Edge of the Forest," translated by Ralph Manheim in *Tiger's Eye* no. 2 (December 1947).

"At the Edge of the Forest," translated by Barbara Wright. *The Trojan Horse and At the Edge of the Forest* (London: Gaberbocchus, 1954).

1. Not an uncommon animal quirk, and one shared by the dog at the beginning of Dostoyevsky's *The Insulted and the Injured*, which Queneau was reading at this time. It indicates, though, the probable origin of Dino's name in the Greek—"dinos": rotation, eddy, an appellation that should make the ending of this piece less baffling to the reader.

2. Gubernatis obviously provides the sense of "gubernatorial" (of or relating to a governor), but it also bears a resemblance to what Christopher Shorley describes in *Queneau's Fiction* as a favorite word of Queneau's: "abrutis" [stunned, dazed, idiot, moron].

Bens proposes the possibility that Queneau is making a reference to Pierre Mendès-France, who had also been a radical socialist and the youngest deputy of France ("À la limite d'un roman"); to what end, however, would be another question.

3. Desnouettes is the name of the square in which Queneau and his wife lived.

4. At the end of the 1930s, Queneau was giving serious thought to becoming a freemason. Alain Calame claims this to have been a result of Guénon's influence.

In Passing

"En passant" was written in the early 1940s, published in *L'Arbalète* no. 8 (spring 1944), and first staged in 1947 at the *Théâtre Agnès Capri* as the opening piece to a production of Luigi Pirandello's *The Life I Gave You* by La Compagnie des Masques. The set design was by the photographer Brassaï, who used immense photographic enlargements for the production. Queneau mentions in his journal that Brassaï had classified thirty thousand photos for the project. Such diverse scenery recalls the cinema, a medium with which Queneau seemed much more in tune than with the theater (he did in fact work on several screenplays, including a film with Luis Buñuel).

Philippe Soupault gave its opening a positive review in *Le Monde illustré*: "One never knows if one should laugh or if one should cry. But what is particularly striking is the cruelty of the author, who shoves his characters about and denounces them pitilessly to the audience . . . A good debut, despite everything, and one that makes one hope that M. Raymond Queneau continues to write for the theater." This "mirror play" (as Emmanuël Souchier calls it; *Raymond Queneau* [Paris: Éditions du Seuil, 1991]), however, turned out to be one of Queneau's only forays into theatrical writing.

Its character pairings and double structure recalls that of Queneau's later novel, *The Blue Flowers*, whose two main characters dream each other into existence. One half of this couple, the bargeman Cidrolin, at one point muses: "How many passersby are there? The fact is there're a lot more passers-by than there need be, or else it's the same passer-by who reverberates from day to day" (trans. Barbara Wright [New York: New Directions, 1985], p. 60).

1. A play on a line from Victor Hugo's "Booz endormi": "C'était l'heure tranquille où les lions vont boire." Queneau played on this verse throughout his works; for more examples, the reader can refer to Souchier, *Raymond Queneau*, p. 167–68.

2. "Le balai": slang for the last train, but literally, a "broom," one of Queneau's favored devices.

3. Another play on Hugo's verse.

Alice in France

Written in 1945 but not published until 1975 in *L'Herne*'s special issue on Queneau, "Alice en France" is something of an effort at children's literature and resembles "At the Forest's Edge" in that its ellipses indicate that it was an aborted project. Anne Clancier refers to this tale as an "exercise in style"—in this case, the style of Queneau's fellow mathematician, Lewis Carroll ("Du fantastique chez Queneau et Vian" in *Trois fous du language: Vian, Queneau, Prévert*, Marc Lapprand, ed. [Nancy: Presses universitaires, 1993]). *Alice in Wonderland* was, in fact, one of Queneau's favorite books, and one he reread throughout his life.

Souchier (*Raymond Queneau*) points out that this text develops itself through the nonsense derived from popular sayings of the time: the comment on everyone not being able to eat white bread, for instance, might make less sense these days given our current predilections for the extra nutrition found in whole grain breads. During wartime, though, refined flour was considered a luxury.

Pierrot is a classic French pantomine character who almost always appears with a whitened face and loose white clothes and is often associated with the moon. He was famously portrayed this same year by Marcel Marceau in the film *Les Enfants du Paradise (Children of Paradise)*. The ending of this piece develops out of the old French song: "Au clair de la lune, mon ami Pierrot, / Prête-moi ta plume pour écrire un mot / Ma chandelle est morte, je n'ai plus de feu / Ouvre-moi ta porte, pour l'amour de Dieu." (In the moonlight, my friend Pierrot, / Lend me your quill to write a word / My candle is out, I've no more fire / Open your door, for the love of God.) This same song provides the title to one of Queneau's better-known novels, as well as a model for the opening of his poem "Souvenir" (in *Le Chien à la mandoline* [Paris: Gallimard, 1965]).

The Café de la France

"Le Café de la France" was written in 1947 and published in *Les Temps modernes* 2, 17 (February 1947). It is a bleak portrait of postwar Havre, which recalls a line from *Saint Glinglin:* "man fulfills himself only in the city." Such fulfillment makes for a melancholic fate, though, when the city fulfills itself as ruins. One might also think of Queneau's early poem "L'Amphion," his hymn to the restless changes of the city; but even more so of "Le Havre de grâce," this piece's equivalent in verse: "Plans shall redraw this topography / Archives shall create this chronology." But what does one do with the ruins? Queneau concludes the poem by evoking the act of sweeping: "A broom a broom for all the dust," leaving one to wonder whether man's fulfillment isn't in the complete vanishing alluded to at the end of *The Last Days*.

PREVIOUS TRANSLATION:
"Café de la France," translated by Brigitte Lambert in *Atlas Anthology* no. 2 (London: Atlas Press, 1984).

1. Queneau recounts this same moment in *The Last Days* (p. 35). This allusion to the past is not arbitrary; one can recall the opening of *Odile*, when he says that "of my first twenty years, only ruins are left in a memory devastated by unhappiness" (trans. Carol Sanders [Normal IL: Dalkey Archive Press, 1988], p. 3).

2. Queneau is probably referring to his 1939 novel, *A Hard Winter*, which is set in Le Havre during the first world war.

3. Armand Salacrou, the French absurdist dramatist, was one of the members of the Academie Goncourt to elect Queneau into their ranks. The two had both been raised in Le Havre.

Green with Fright
Written and published in 1947 by Éditions de Minuit under its own title, "Une trouille verte" was accompanied by "Dino" and "Panic." Although a dream account of sorts, this text reads more obviously as a dig at the postwar existentialists then in vogue in general, and at Jean-Paul Sartre in particular, with whom Queneau was on friendly terms. The famous chestnut tree from that author's *Nausea* here takes the form of a chestnut purée. Although "nothingness" was very much in style at this time, (largely due to Heidegger's influence and Sartre's *Being and Nothingness*), the "presence" and reality of such a creature had been a point of interest to Queneau as early as his first novel, *The Bark Tree*. In that book, he provided something of a kernel to his narrative through a Heideggerian rewriting of Plato's *The Sophist*, recognizing the fact that "being is determined by nonbeing" (trans. Barbara Wright [New York: New Directions, 1971], p. 244).

The title is a play on words: to have a "peur bleue" is to be scared stiff, but literally, to have a "blue fear"; to be "vert de peur" is, again, to be scared out of your wits, but literally, to be "green with fear"; to have a "trouille" is to be scared to death; adding color to it only makes for silliness.

PREVIOUS TRANSLATION:
"A Blue Funk," translated by Barbara Wright in *French Writing Today*, Simon Watson Taylor, ed. (New York: Grove, 1969).

The Trojan Horse
Le Cheval troyen was written in 1948 and published the same year as a book by Éditions Georges Visat. Another somewhat snobbish mammal (Queneau's characters

like mentioning their pedigrees), this story is actually based on a real-life incident. As Jacques Bens first told it, the tale took place with a black man; Queneau, fearing he would be suspected of racism, changed the character into a horse (*Temps mêlés: Documents Queneau* no. 150+17–18–19 [April 1983]).

PREVIOUS TRANSLATION:
"The Trojan Horse," translated by Barbara Wright in *The Trojan Horse and At the Edge of the Forest* (London: Gaberbocchus, 1954).

 1. The Houyhnhnms are a race of horses in Jonathan Swift's *Gulliver's Travels*, superior to humans (or "Yahoos") in every aspect. The word's etymology, explains Gulliver, signifies "the perfection of nature." In the interest of this story, it should be noted that for the Houyhnhnms death (or *shnuwnh*: "to retire to one's first mother"), is an event to be greeted or experienced without regret or remorse.

Preface to Book of Cocktails
"Préface au *Livre de Cocktails* d'Émile Bauwens" was written and published in 1949 (Brussels: Un Coup de dés). So that the reader may not be deprived of a bad pun, it would perhaps help to know that a "cocktail" (which normally has this American spelling in French, not Queneau's Frenchified version) refers not only to the drinks of that denomination, but also to a horse who has had its tail docked.

On the Proper Use of Tranquilizers
"(Du bon emploi des tranquillisants), I, II" constitutes three of five sketches that were written sometime in the 1950s, but not published until 1979 in *Temps mêlés: Documents Queneau* no. 150+4 (May 1979). The first two were combined into one for Gallimard's publication of this volume, and are presented as such here, although it seems questionable that this had been Queneau's intent. All five were humorous replies to a publicity campaign of the H. Baille laboratories. Tranquilizers had been recently introduced to the general public at that time; the best-known major tranquilizer, Chlorpromazine, was first synthesized in France in 1950; its first application was in 1952.

 1. Arcole and Moscow were battles fought by Napoleon I in 1796 and 1812, respectively; Magenta and Reichshoffen by Napoleon III in 1859 and 1870. The speaker is not only a veteran of all four wars, but probably disfigured by them as well: the Avenue de Tourville in Paris is where the Hôtel des Invalides is located.

Auguste Nélaton (1807–73) was a French surgeon, senator and member of the Institute of France; he became surgeon to Napoleon III in 1866. One of the most common battlefield operations of that time was amputation, which provided the most clear-cut government guidelines for veteran disability recompensation, something that was graduated according to seriousness of disability. Thus two amputated or useless limbs earned greater recompensation and sympathy than one.

Amputated limbs were often replaced with wooden ones. A veteran with a wooden head, then, would no doubt have garnered top respect. Such a character was a more common joke in the past; Henri Rousseau's play *A Visit to the Exposition of 1889*, for instance, presents several country bumpkins paying a visit to the Hôtel des Invalides in the hopes of seeing this wooden-headed soldier.

2. "Le petit tondu" (literally, "little baldy" or "little short-back-and-sides") was a nickname for Napoleon Bonaparte.

The Aerodynamic Properties of Addition

Written and published in the first issue of the *Cahiers du Collège de 'Pataphysique* in 1950 (15 clinamen 77 [6 April 1950]), the year Queneau was officially elected as one of their satraps, "Quelque remarques sommaires relatives aux propriétés aérodynamiques de l'addition" is perhaps his earliest written contribution to the College.

Queneau was a member of the Société mathématique de France at the time of writing this piece. A year later, he wrote and spoke the commentary for a short film by Pierre Kast entitled "Arithmetique," a nine minute exposition made for an "Encyclopedia on film" and screened on television in 1953. Something of a disciple of Pythagoras, Queneau once claimed that mathematics are "the very structure of the human spirit" (quoted by Simonnet, *Queneau déchiffré*, p. 65).

PREVIOUS TRANSLATION:
"A Few Summary Remarks Relative to the Aerodynamic Properties of Addition," translated by Simon Watson Taylor in *The London Broadsheet* no.3 (March 1955).

Conversations in Greater Paris

Queneau assembled, in chronological order, "Conversations dans le département de la Seine" from various notations he made in his journals from 1949 to 1956, with only occasional omissions and slight changes in punctuation. It was published as a whole in 1962 in the summer issue of *L'Arc* (Aix-en-Provence) 5, 19. Although it takes the form of a document more than that of a poem, one could see the precedent for this text in some of Apollinaire's poetry, particularly "Lundi rue Christine," which is composed entirely of overheard conversation in a cafe. The historical information I've footnoted for this piece I owe to A. I. Queneau, the editor of Queneau's recently published journals.

1. The Petiot affair: A criminal trial that took place in 1946. Doctor Petiot (1893–1946) was condemned to death and executed for having committed twenty-seven murders between 1942 and 1944 in a Parisian hotel.

2. A "parenthesis" can also, in French slang, refer to the female genitals.

3. Michel Cerdan: a boxer beaten in 1949 by La Motta. He died the same year in a plane crash as he was heading off to rewin his title.

4. *La Grève des Forgerons* (The blacksmith's strike): A. I. Queneau feels that this refers to a book by Lucien Dubech (1926), not to the better-known poem by François Coppée (1869).

5. The Dalloz: A series of dictionaries, law manuals, and other technical publications.

6. Coccinelle: a female impersonator famous in his time.

7. Queneau left out a line here from the monologue as he had recorded it in his journal: "Well, I tell them, I do striptize every morning in front of my mirror."

8. In the recording Queneau made of this text in his journals, [Bernard] "Buffet" is [Jean] "Dubuffet."

Manners of Speaking

"Façons de parler" was written in 1963 and published as part of an album: *Pour Daniel-Henry Kahnweiler* (Stuggart: Verlag Gerd Hatje, 1965).

The names are somewhat comic sounding in Greek and manage to situate the characters before they even open their mouths. "Melanopyge" translates as "stained in black," whereas "Aristenete" has the same root as "aristocracy."

1. Queneau is citing a verse from Guillaume Apollinaire's poem "Marie": "Je passais au bord de la Seine / Un livre ancien sous le bras."

Texticles

Queneau wrote and published these "Texticules" beginning in 1949. They were published as a whole in a limited edition by Galerie Louise Leiris in Paris, 1968. The title alone (one also used by Marcel Duchamp) indicates that Queneau did not count any of these texts among his major works—which doesn't prevent them from making for a bewildering read. Sarane Alexandrian, one of the few critics to even mention their existence, refers to these pieces as prose poems (in her book on Surrealist authors, *Le Surréalisme et le rêve*), but such an appellation falls short of accounting for their oddness. Most of them read like puzzles, either playing on popular sayings or taking puns without the usual grain of salt. A few, such as "Cosmophilia" or "Portrait of a Certain Joe Schmoe," may be rooted in a source text that Queneau had manipulated. Nearly all of them, even when Queneau's particular game or method is evident, make for frustrating translation, and some wordplay has unavoidably perished in the linguistic crossing.

1. This dialogue develops out of two French expressions: "l'ogre aime la chair fraîche" ("the ogre likes a diet of warm young flesh"); and "l'entendre de mes oreilles de chair" ("to hear with my own ears," but literally, "to hear with my ears of flesh").

2. This text recalls Queneau's very early "Surrealist Text," in which a "stranger" bends the letter "I" into an "A," and thus turns an "isthme" (isthmus) into an "asthme" (asthma).

3. Queneau is playing on the opening verses of Victor Hugo's poem, "Oceano Nox": "Oh! combien de marins, combien de capitaines / Qui sont partis joyeux pour des courses lointaines, / Dans ce morne horizon se sont évanouis!" (Oh, how many sailors, how many captains / Who had joyously left for faroff journeys, / Disappeared in this dreary horizon!)

4. Of all the makers of pens buried in this text, the "sergent-major" will probably be the least familiar to the English reader; it was, however, Queneau's favorite brand, and the only one he would use.

5. I'm again indebted to Madeleine Velguth for pointing out the buried pun fueling this little text: "pénicilline" (penicillin): "peine, ici, Line" (penalty, here, Line).

6. An untranslatable pun. Whereas the "langue d'oïl" and the "langue d'oc" actually exist, the "langue d'oust" is Queneau's own creation, which enables the concluding pun: "Langouste mayonnaise" is a popular French dish—crayfish in mayonnaise; "langue oust bayonnaise" would be a langue d'oust from Bayonne.

7. An echo of the opening of Charles Baudelaire's "Recueillement": "Sois sage ô ma douleur, et tiens-toi plus tranquille." (Behave yourself O my pain, and be quieter.)

8. In French: "les échos qu'aux cocoricos"; for another English equivalent, one could ask: "some coke or cocoa, Rico?"

9. In French, an "enraged sheep" ("mouton enragé") is a normally placid person who suddenly explodes in a fit of violent anger.

10. This text originally belonged to another of Queneau's collections of minor texts, "Foutaises," which eventually became the endpiece to *Les Œuvres complètes de Sally Mara*: "Sally plus intime."

11. One hundred "ouiches" (or "cent d'ouiches") in French provides the phonetic equivalent of a "sandwich."

A Story of Your Own

"Un conte à votre façon" was written in 1967, presented at the eighty-third meeting of the Oulipo, and published in *Les Lettres Nouvelles* (July–September) that same year. After his *100,000,000,000,000 Poems,* this is perhaps Queneau's best known textual contribution to the Oulipo and an early example of permutative methods derived from computer flow charts to be applied to a literary text. A visual rendition of the story can be found in Warren F. Motte's *Oulipo,* p. 121, which gives an indication of the difficulties involved in constructing such texts. An interactive reading of the story was created for the computer under the auspices of ARTA (Atelier Recherches Techniques Avancées).

The idea of "tree" literature had been proposed by François Le Lionnais at the seventy-ninth meeting of the Oulipo. The form would eventually develop into the better known "Choose your own adventure" books for adolescents.

All in all, though, Queneau's story reads as much as a parody as a serious exploration of the form, since more than one of the reader's options turn out not to be options at all, and several selections (such as the very last one), are phrased in such a way as to assume that the reader had already read the alternative selection. Perec's own algorithmic work, the theatrical *L'Augmentation,* which he wrote a couple of years later, capitalizes on this element: rather than allow the reader (or viewer) a participatory involvement, he instead plays out every possible permutation for the audience, mocking the futility of choice in the bureaucratic structure he portrays.

PREVIOUS TRANSLATIONS:

Yours for the Telling, translated by John Crombie (Paris: Kickshaws, 1982).

"A Story as You Like It," translated and edited by Warren F. Motte Jr. *Oulipo: A Primer of Potential Literature* (Normal IL: The Dalkey Archive, 1998).

1. Homer's classic utterance when he is on the verge of relating something of import; the best translation of such a cry that I've come across would be the Yiddish "Oy vey!" proposed by my uncle.

On Some Imaginary Animal Languages
"De quelque langages animaux imaginaires et notamment du langage chien dans *Sylvie et Bruno*" was written and published on its own in 1971 by Éditions de l'Herne in their "l'Envers" collection. Although of obvious interest given Queneau's fabular bent, animal languages were a subject to arise in more than one Oulipo meeting: on 1 July 1963, François Le Lionnais first proposed the writing of animal poetry, using only those human sounds that are understood by certain animals. A dog poem, then, as defined in the *Oulipo Compendium*, is "A poem that incorporates a dog's name in such a way that it remains hidden to the human eye but audible to the canine ear" (Harry Mathews and Alastair Brotchie, eds. [London: Atlas Press, 1998], p. 136). French and English examples of this form have been written by François Caradec and Harry Mathews. Another Oulipian, Jacques Jouet, composed a number of poems in "Great-Ape"—a language created by Edgar Rice Burroughs for his Tarzan series.

Queneau's own semiserious interest in the notion, though, is evident as early as 1952; a note in his journal of that time reads: "lecture by Kojève—*Against* animal languages: they don't ask questions" (*Journaux*, p. 779).

In this piece, the "base" and "ignoble" nature of the dog is elevated (as is so much of Queneau's subject matter) through an attention and style usually reserved for "nobler" matters.

1. George Psalmanazar, whose real name is unknown, was, after Daniel Defoe, one of the more famous "Travel Liars" of the eighteenth century. Erudite in his youth, Psalmanazar later pretended he had visited the island of Formosa and invented the language he claimed to have learned from a native there. He allowed himself to be converted back to Christianity, attained a position at Oxford teaching future missionaries, and was eventually persuaded to write an account of his travels, in which he stated, among other things, that the Formosans sacrificed eighteen thousand boys under nine years of age every year (Jonathan Swift makes one of the better-known allusions to the "famous Psalmanazar" in his "Modest Proposal"). In later years Psalmanazar repented, led a chaste life, and became a dear friend of Samuel Johnson. For more information on his life, the reader can turn to his *Memoirs* or Percy G. Adams, *Travelers and Travel Liars 1660–1800* (New York: Dover, 1980).

Dream Accounts Aplenty
"Des récits de rêves à foison" was written and published in 1973, in the October issue of *Les Cahiers du Chemin* no. 19. Whereas Queneau's first published piece of writing was a dream account in *La Révolution surréaliste* no. 3 (15 April 1925), this late text was something of a refutation of dream-writing, circling back like a reflection upon this literary debut. Although Queneau made many disparaging remarks concerning

Louis Aragon
The Adventures of Telemachus
Translated by Renée Riese Hubert and Judd D. Hubert

Louis Aragon
Treatise on Style
Translated by Alyson Waters

Marcel Bénabou
Why I Have Not Written Any of My Books
Translated by David Kornacker

Maurice Blanchot
Awaiting Oblivion
Translated by John Gregg

Maurice Blanchot
The Most High
Translated by Allan Stoekl

André Breton
Break of Day
Translated by Mark Polizzotti and Mary Ann Caws

André Breton
Communicating Vessels
Translated by Mary Ann Caws and Geoffrey T. Harris

André Breton
Free Rein
Translated by Michel Parmentier and Jacqueline d'Amboise

André Breton
The Lost Steps
Translated by Mark Polizzotti

André Breton
Mad Love
Translated by Mary Ann Caws

Blaise Cendrars
Modernities and Other Writings
Edited by Monique Chefdor
Translated by Esther Allen and Monique Chefdor

The Cubist Poets in Paris: An Anthology
Edited by L. C. Breunig

René Daumal
You've Always Been Wrong
Translated by Thomas Vosteen

Max Jacob
Hesitant Fire: Selected Prose of Max Jacob
Translated and edited by Moishe Black and Maria Green

Jean Paulhan
Progress in Love on the Slow Side
Translated by Christine Moneera Laennec and Michael Syrotinski

Benjamin Péret
Death to the Pigs, and Other Writings
Translated by Rachel Stella and Others

Surrealist practice throughout the essays of *Le Voyage en Grèce*—attacking automatic writing, their ideas of inspiration and the parlor games for which they were known— the dream account has played a role throughout Queneau's works (most obviously in the entire conclusion of the first part of *The Bark Tree*, and *The Skin of Dreams* as a whole). In a short piece in the artist book, *Monuments*, Queneau claimed that dreams are no longer what they used to be for two reasons: the "vulgarization of psycho- analysis," and the influence of the cinema ("mouvizes"), which also plays a role in many of his novels.

This meditation on dream grammar resulted from his reading of *La Boutique ob- scure*, Georges Perec's account of 124 dreams. Queneau set out to prove a comment he made years before in his essay "L'Air et la chanson," in which he tried to rehabili- tate the notion of "literature": "a bit of lucidity would have shown him [he is here speaking of an "obscure surrealist"] that the posting up of the word 'revolution' was no longer anything but a 'literary' process" (*Le Voyage en Grèce*, p. 65). While not nec- essarily disparaging the dream account itself, Queneau here tries to show that it is a literary *style*: no more, no less.

PREVIOUS TRANSLATION:

"Accounts of Abundant Dreams," translated by Brigitte Lambert in *Atlas Anthology III*, Alastair Brotchie and Malcolm Green, eds. (London: Atlas Press, 1985).

Raymond Queneau
Stories and Remarks
Translated by Marc Lowenthal

Boris Vian
Blues for a Black Cat and Other Stories
Edited and translated by Julia Older